高顿CFA® 祝你备考无忧!

免费赠送1年CFA会员学习权益

- 精选阶段题库
- 复习备考指南
- 金融热点资讯
- 考试入门指导

扫码添加小助手，回复"领会员"即可免费获取一年会员权益！

CFA® 一级 精要图解

Chartered Financial Analyst

高顿教育研究院 ◎ 编著

文汇出版社

图书在版编目（CIP）数据

CFA®一级精要图解．图／高顿教育研究院编著．—上海：文汇出版社，2023.10
ISBN 978-7-5496-4087-4

Ⅰ.①C… Ⅱ.①高… Ⅲ.①金融—分析—资格考试—自学参考资料 Ⅳ.①F83

中国国家版本馆CIP数据核字（2023）第120560号

CFA® 一级精要图解（图）

编　著 /	高顿教育研究院
责任编辑 /	戴　铮
封面设计 /	汤惟惟
版式设计 /	汤惟惟
出版发行 /	**文匯**出版社
	上海市威海路755号
	（邮政编码：200041）
印刷装订 /	上海普顺印刷包装有限公司
版　次 /	2023年10月第1版
印　次 /	2025年8月第3次印刷
开　本 /	787毫米×1092毫米 1/16
字　数 /	53千字
印　张 /	8.25
书　号 /	ISBN 978-7-5496-4087-4
定　价 /	85.00元

前言

谈及 CFA® 考试，许多备考考生都因为这门考试的庞杂知识体系而感到束手无策。CFA® 知识包括 10 门课程，所覆盖的内容包含职业伦理道德、分析工具，金融产品和投资组合四大知识模块。初次接触 CFA® 的考生，往往会"迷失"在其庞杂而精碎的知识海洋中，从而难以跳出具体知识点，以更好的框架感俯视每门课程的知识体系。这种"只见树木不见森林"的学习，既使得考生学习和记忆的难度大幅增加，也造成了所学无法应用的困窘。

为解决大家学习过程中的这个"痛点"，高顿教育研究院秉承"靶向教学"与"体系性"两大传统，历经五年打磨，为广大考生精心编纂了《CFA® 一级精要图解（图）》和《CFA® 一级精要图解（文）》。我们希望这套书能作为 CFA® 考生的"知识地图"：让大家在学习具体知识点时，能够清晰判断出该知识点"身在何处"，能更准确地找到该知识点与其他知识点的关系。通过更清晰的"路标"，我们希望能帮助各位考生掌握 CFA® 知识，又能助力大家高效备考。

《CFA® 一级精要图解（图）》旨在为考生搭建知识整体框架，将繁杂无序的知识点以"脑图"形式呈现给考生，帮助加深理解、强化记忆。而《CFA® 一级精要图解（文）》则是对《CFA® 一级精要图解（图）》的展开和具体讲解，聚焦知识点的解读，方便考生查漏补缺、掌握核心考点。中英文对照的呈现方式，在紧贴英文考试的同时，也方便中国考生理解和记忆。

基于十多年的教学研究和经验积累，我们将知识点分为：重点掌握，掌握和了解三大类。在"知识图谱"中，★ 代表重点掌握，⭐ 代表掌握，而未标星级的则代表了解。我们对重要知识点着以绿色底色，方便考生迅速定位重要考点，同时将文字转化为简洁清晰的图形。书中涉及的图标及其具体含义如下表所示：

图 标	含 义
⊕	正相关（同向关系）
⊖	负相关（反向关系）
!	特别注意
✖	禁止／不适用
▶	允许／适用于

今年新增了"预备知识"模块，该模块下的知识为非考纲内容，但为考纲知识点密切相关，故将其作为考纲知识点的学习基础或与考纲知识点密切相关，放在正文的前面。

有相关基础的考生可以跳过此模块，其他考生可以阅读本模块内容，以更好地理解正文中的考纲知识内容。

本套书适用于三类学习场景：课前预习、课后复习以及考前冲刺。

课前预习——在备考初期，本套书可作为知识引导，让考生对每个章节的内容有大致了解。

课后复习——每完成一个章节的学习后，考生可将本书作为一个自查清单，检验学习效果。

考前冲刺——本套书作为知识点的精炼总结，可以帮助考生快速复习重要知识点。

本套书的章节顺序与高顿教育研究院出版的《CFA® 一级中文教材》保持一致，方便考生对照查询相关知识点的详细讲解。

另外，我们也会根据考纲及时更新《CFA® 一级精要图解（图）》和《CFA® 一级精要图解（文）》的相关内容，确保内容与最新考纲完全一致。

本套书凝聚了高顿教育研究院百位讲师和研究员十多年的教学研究成果，我们衷心希望本套书能帮助广大考生取得更好的成绩，顺利通过考试！

高顿教育研究院

目录

第一部分 数量分析方法 ... 1

- Reading 1 The Time Value of Money ... 2
- Reading 2 Statistics Measures of Asset Returns ... 4
- Reading 3 Probability Concepts ... 6
- Reading 4 Common Probability Distributions ... 7
- Reading 5 Estimation and Inference ... 8
- Reading 6 Hypothesis Testing ... 9
- Reading 7 Introduction to Linear Regression ... 10
- Reading 8 Introduction to Big Data Techniques ... 12

第二部分 经济学 ... 13

- Reading 9 Firm and Market Structures ... 14
- Reading 10 Understanding Business Cycles ... 16
- Reading 11 Fiscal and Monetary Policy ... 18
- Reading 12 International Trade ... 20
- Reading 13 Capital Flows and the FX Market ... 21
- Reading 14 Exchange Rate Calculations ... 22
- Reading 15 Introduction to Geopolitics ... 23

第三部分 财务报表分析 25

Reading 16　Introduction to Financial Statement Analysis 26
Reading 17　Analyzing Income Statements 28
Reading 18　Analyzing Balance Sheets 30
Reading 19　Analyzing Statements of Cash Flows 31
Reading 20　Financial Analysis Techniques 32
Reading 21　Analysis of Inventories 34
Reading 22　Analysis of Long-Term Assets 36
Reading 23　Topics in Long-Term Liabilities and Equity 38
Reading 24　Analysis of Income Taxes 40
Reading 25　Financial Reporting Quality 41
Reading 26　Introduction to Financial Statement Modeling 42

第四部分 公司发行人 43

Reading 27　Organizational Forms, Corporate Issuer Feature, and Ownership 44
Reading 28　Investors and Other Stakeholders 45
Reading 29　Corporate Governance: Conflicts, Mechanisms, Risks, and Benefits 46
Reading 30　Business Models 47
Reading 31　Working Capital & Liquidity 48
Reading 32　Capital Investments and Capital Allocation 50
Reading 33　Capital Structure 52

第五部分 权益投资 … 55

- Reading 34　Market Organization and Structure … 56
- Reading 35　Security Market Indexes … 59
- Reading 36　Market Efficiency … 60
- Reading 37　Overview of Equity Securities … 62
- Reading 38　Introduction to Industry and Company Analysis … 64
- Reading 39　Equity Valuation: Concepts and Basic Tools … 66

第六部分 固定收益证券 … 69

- Reading 40　Fixed-Income Securities … 70
- Reading 41　Fixed-Income Markets … 74
- Reading 42　Fixed-Income Valuation … 76
- Reading 43　Interest Rate Risk … 78
- Reading 44　Credit Risk … 80
- Reading 45　Asset-Backed Security … 82

第七部分 衍生品 … 85

- Reading 46　Derivative Markets and Instruments … 86
- Reading 47　Basics of Derivative Pricing and Valuation … 90

第八部分 另类投资 … 95

- Reading 48　Basic Concepts of Alternative Investments … 96
- Reading 49　Asset Types of Alternative Investments … 97

第九部分 投资组合管理 ······101

- Reading 50　Portfolio Management: An Overview ······102
- Reading 51　Portfolio Risk and Return: Part I ······104
- Reading 52　Portfolio Risk and Return: Part II ······106
- Reading 53　Basics of Portfolio Planning and Construction ······108
- Reading 54　The Behavioral Biases of Individuals ······110
- Reading 55　Introduction to Risk Management ······112

第十部分 伦理与职业标准 ······115

- Reading 56　Ethics and Trust in the Investment Profession ······116
- Reading 57　Code of Ethics and Standards of Professional Conduct ······117
- Reading 58　Guidance for Standards I – VII ······118
- Reading 59　Introduction to the Global Investment Performance Standards (GIPS) ······122
- Reading 60　Ethics Application ······123

第一部分 数量分析方法

Reading 1　The Time Value of Money

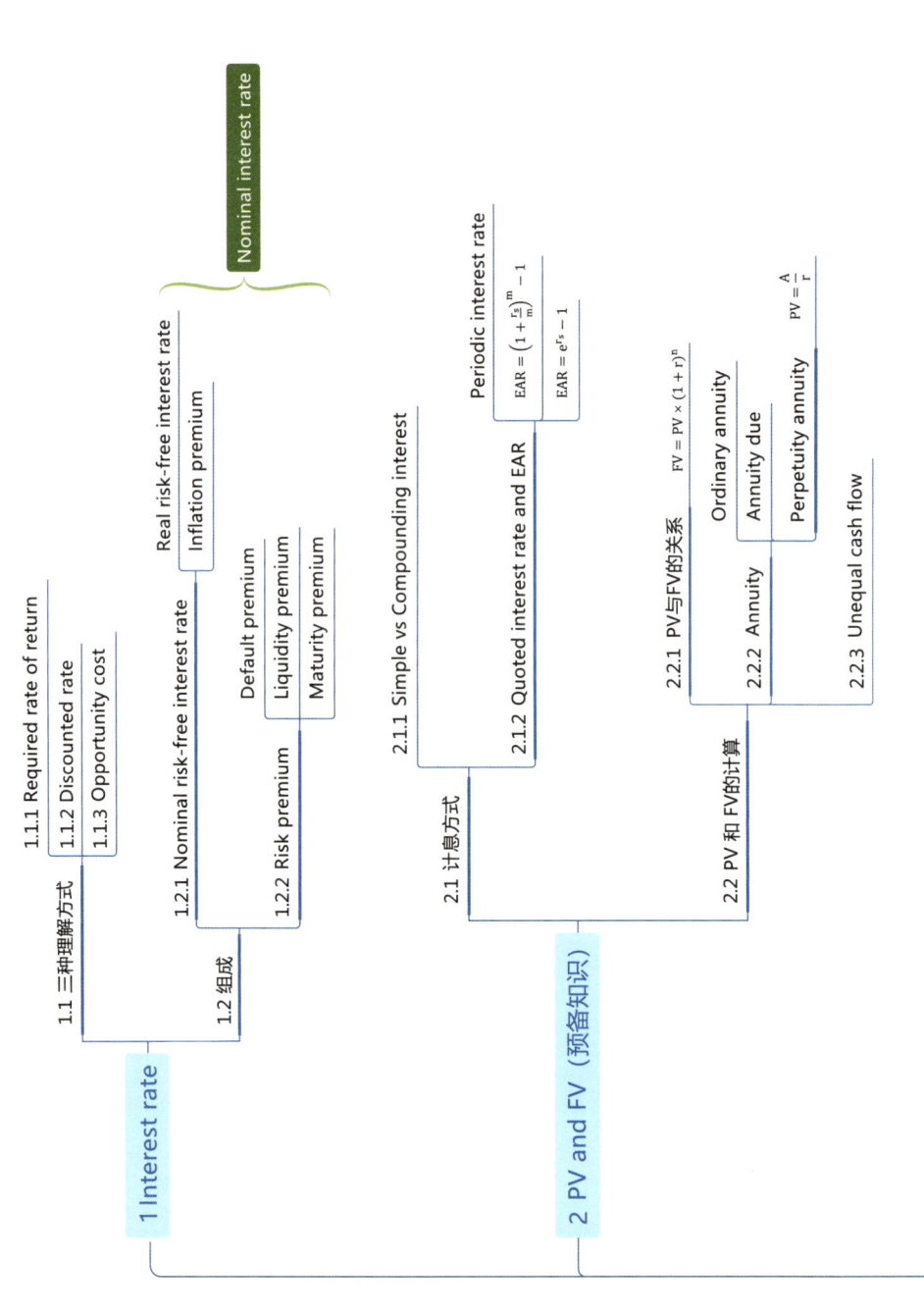

3 Rates of return

3.1 ★ Holding period return

- 3.1.1 HPR $= \frac{P_T + I_T}{P_0} - 1$
- 3.1.2 Annualized return: $R_{annual} = (1 + R_{period})^c - 1$
- 3.1.3 Continuously compounded return: $r_{t,t+1} = \ln\left(\frac{P_{t+1}}{P_t}\right) = \ln(1 + R_{t,t+1})$

3.2 Average return

- 3.2.1 ★ Arithmetic mean return
- 3.2.2 ★ Geometric mean return: $\overline{R}_G = \sqrt[n]{(1 + R_1)(1 + R_2)\cdots(1 + R_n)} - 1$
- 3.2.3 ★ Harmonic mean return: $\overline{X}_{Harmonic} = \dfrac{N}{\sum_{i=1}^{N}\frac{1}{X_i}}$

{ 三者大小关系 }

- 3.2.4 ★ MWR: $CF_0 + \dfrac{CF_1}{1 + MWR} + \dfrac{CF_2}{(1 + MWR)^2} + \cdots + \dfrac{CF_N}{(1 + MWR)^N} = 0$
- 3.2.5 ★ TWR: $TWR = [(1 + HPR_1) \times (1 + HPR_2) \times \cdots \times (1 + HPR_n)]^{\frac{1}{N}} - 1$

{ MWR与TWR之间的关系 }

3.3 Other major returns

- 3.3.1 Gross and net return
- 3.3.2 Pre-tax and after-tax return
- 3.3.3 Real return: $(1 + \text{real return}) = \dfrac{(1 + \text{nominal risk free rate})(1 + \text{risk premium})}{1 + \text{inflation premium}}$
- 3.3.4 ★ Leveraged return: $R_L = R_P + \dfrac{V_B}{V_E}(R_P - r_D)$

Reading 2　Statistics Measures of Asset Returns

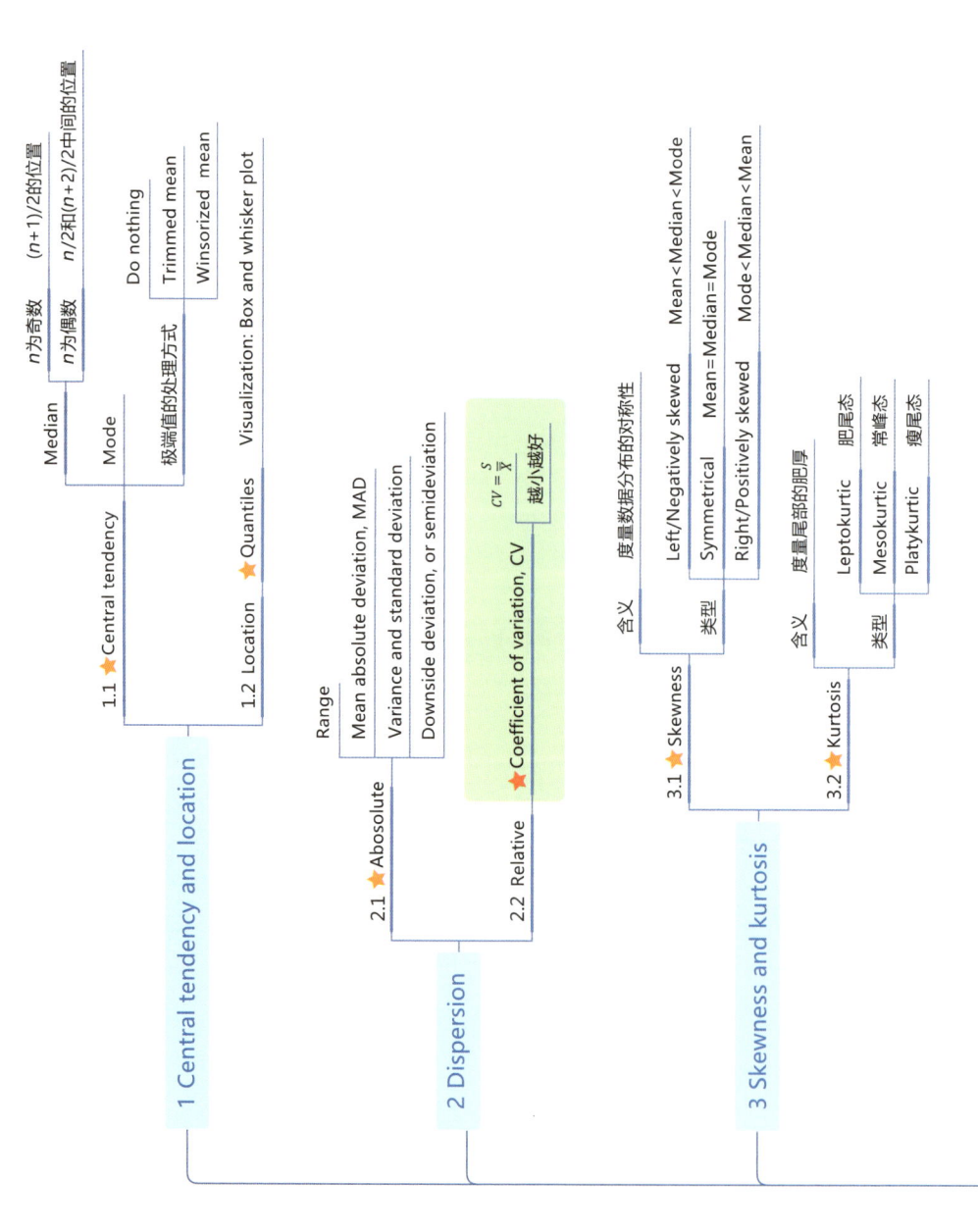

4 Covariance and correlation

4.1 ★ Covariance

- **含义**: 度量两个随机变量变化的方向性
- **计算**: $S_{XY} = \dfrac{\sum_{i=1}^{n}(X_i - \overline{X})(Y_i - \overline{Y})}{n-1}$
- **性质**:
  - 取值范围 $(-\infty, +\infty)$
  - 大于0, X和Y同向变化
  - 小于0, X和Y反向变化

4.2 ★ Correlation

- **含义**: 度量两个随机变化的线性关系
- **计算**: $r_{XY} = \dfrac{S_{XY}}{S_X S_Y}$
- **性质**:
  - 取值范围 $[-1, +1]$
  - 等于-1, 完美的负线性关系
  - -1与0之间, 负的线性关系; 绝对值越大, 线性关系越强
  - 等于0, 没有线性关系 (不代表没有其他关系)
  - 0与+1之间, 正的线性关系; 绝对值越大, 线性关系越强
  - 等于+1, 完美的正线性关系
- **局限性**:
  - 对极端值非常敏感
  - 相关性不意味着因果关系
  - 伪相关

Reading 3　Probability Concepts

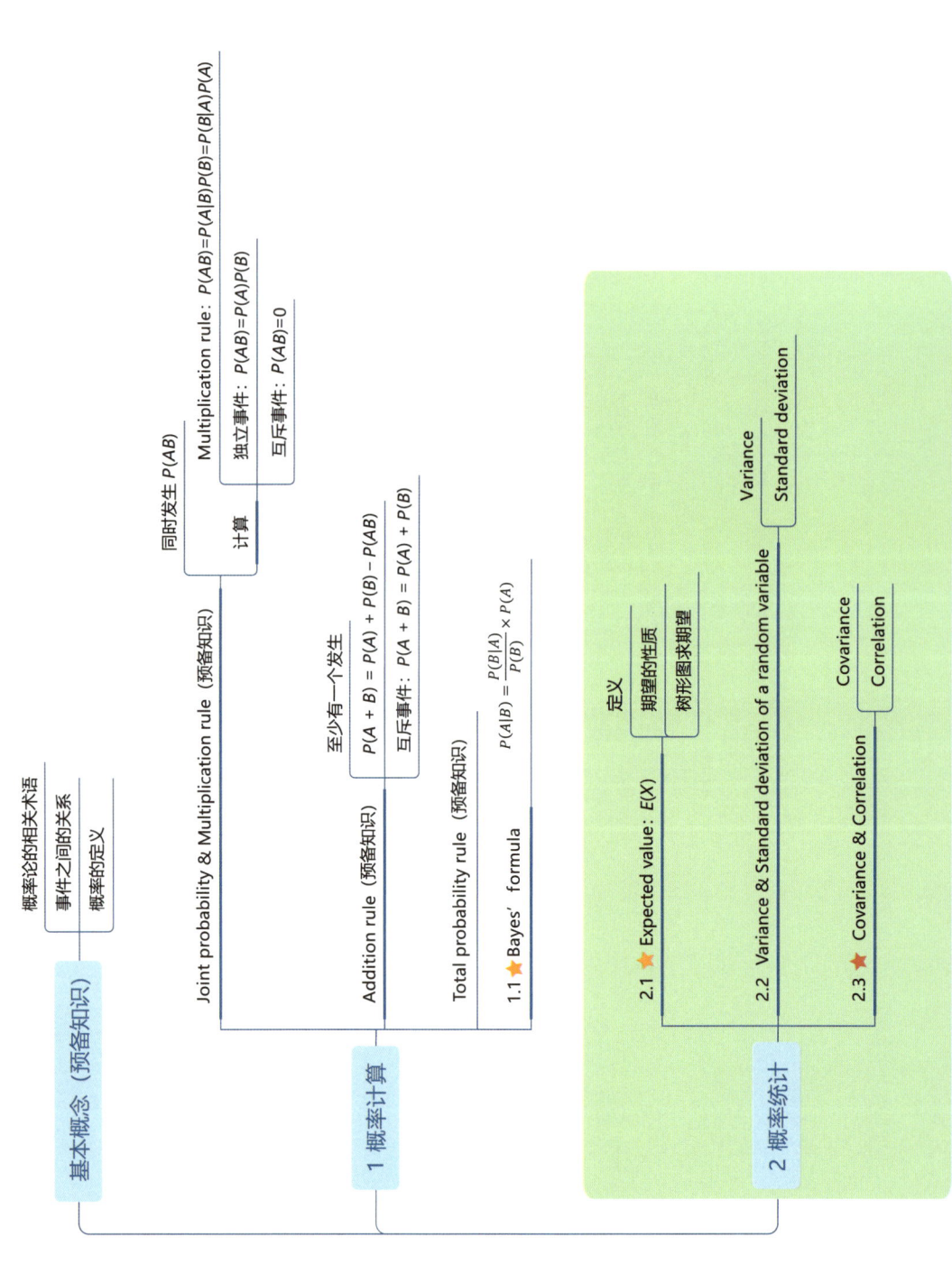

Reading 4　Common Probability Distributions

- 基础概念（预备知识）
  - Discrete vs Continuous random variables
    - Discrete random variable — 可数
    - Continuous random variable — 无限 + 不可数
  - Distribution function
    - 概率密度函数（Probability density function, PDF）
      - Probability function, PF
      - Cumulative distribution function, CDF

- 1 Continuous distribution
  - Normal distribution（预备知识）
    - 正态分布的概念与性质
      - Standard normal distribution
  - Student's t-distribution（预备知识）
  - Chi-square distribution and F-distribution（预备知识）
  - **1.1 ★ Application of normal distribution**
    - **Shortfall risk**
    - **Roy's safety first ratio**
  - **1.2 Lognormal distribution**

Reading 5　Estimation and Inference

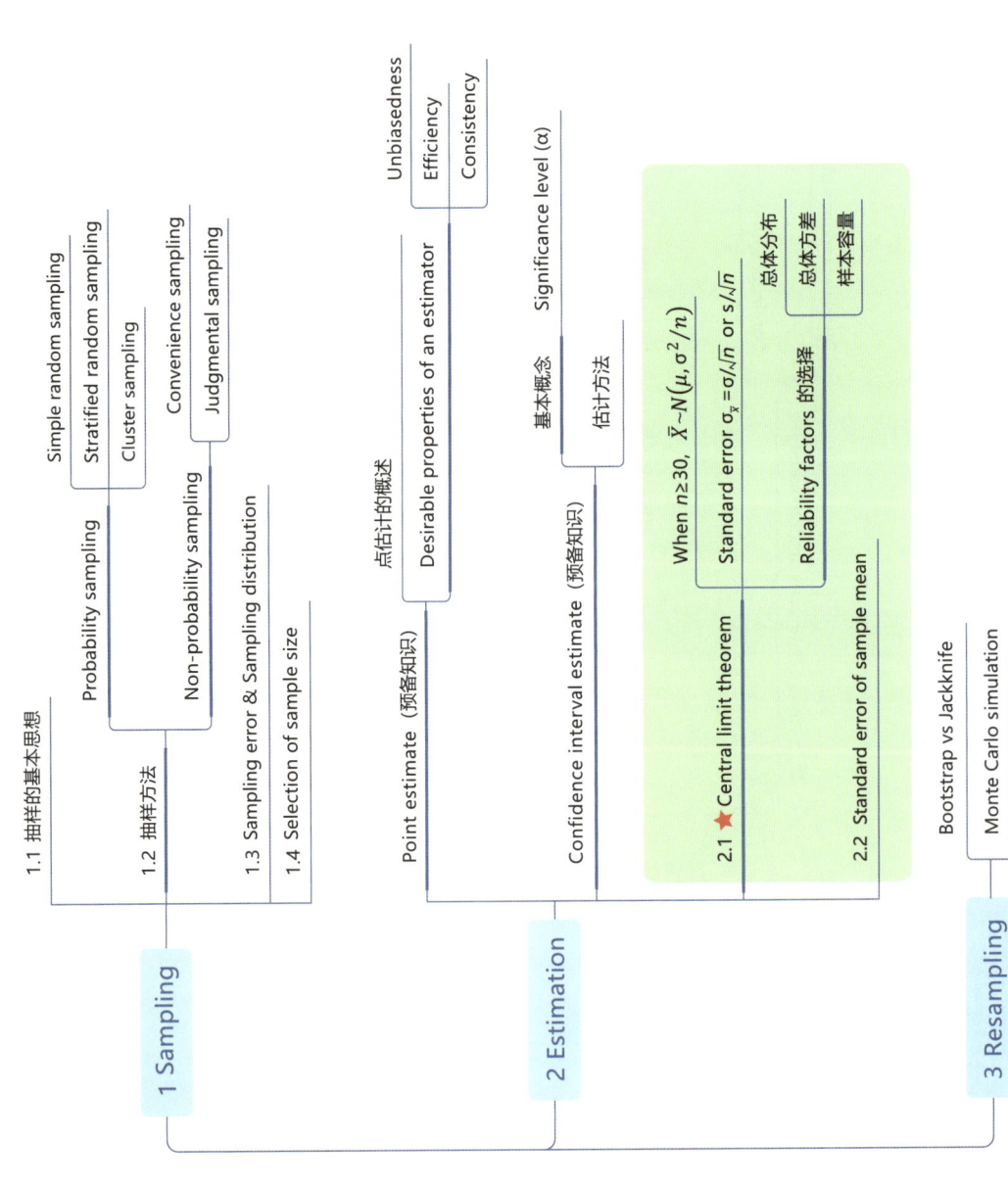

Reading 6　Hypothesis Testing

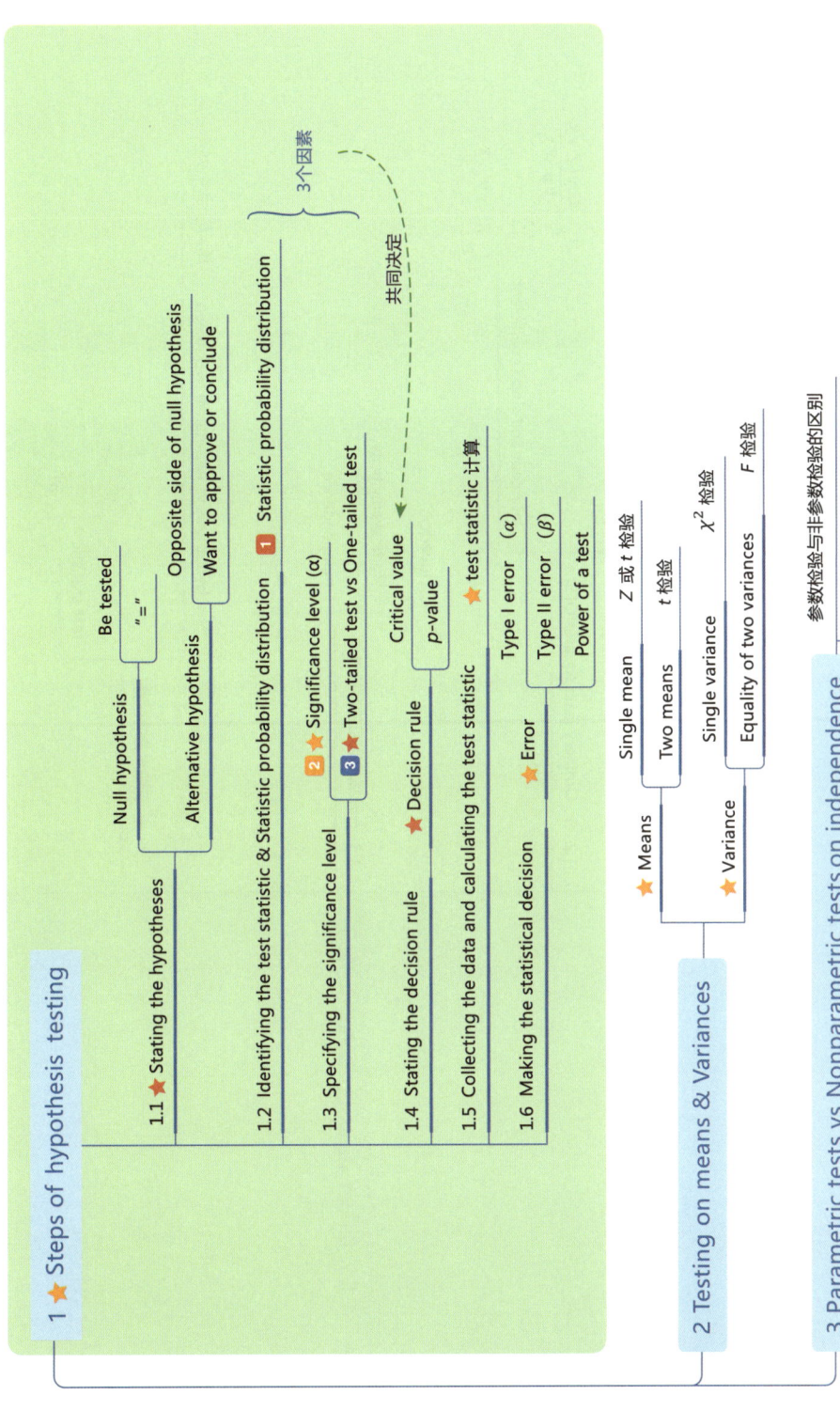

Reading 7 Introduction to Linear Regression

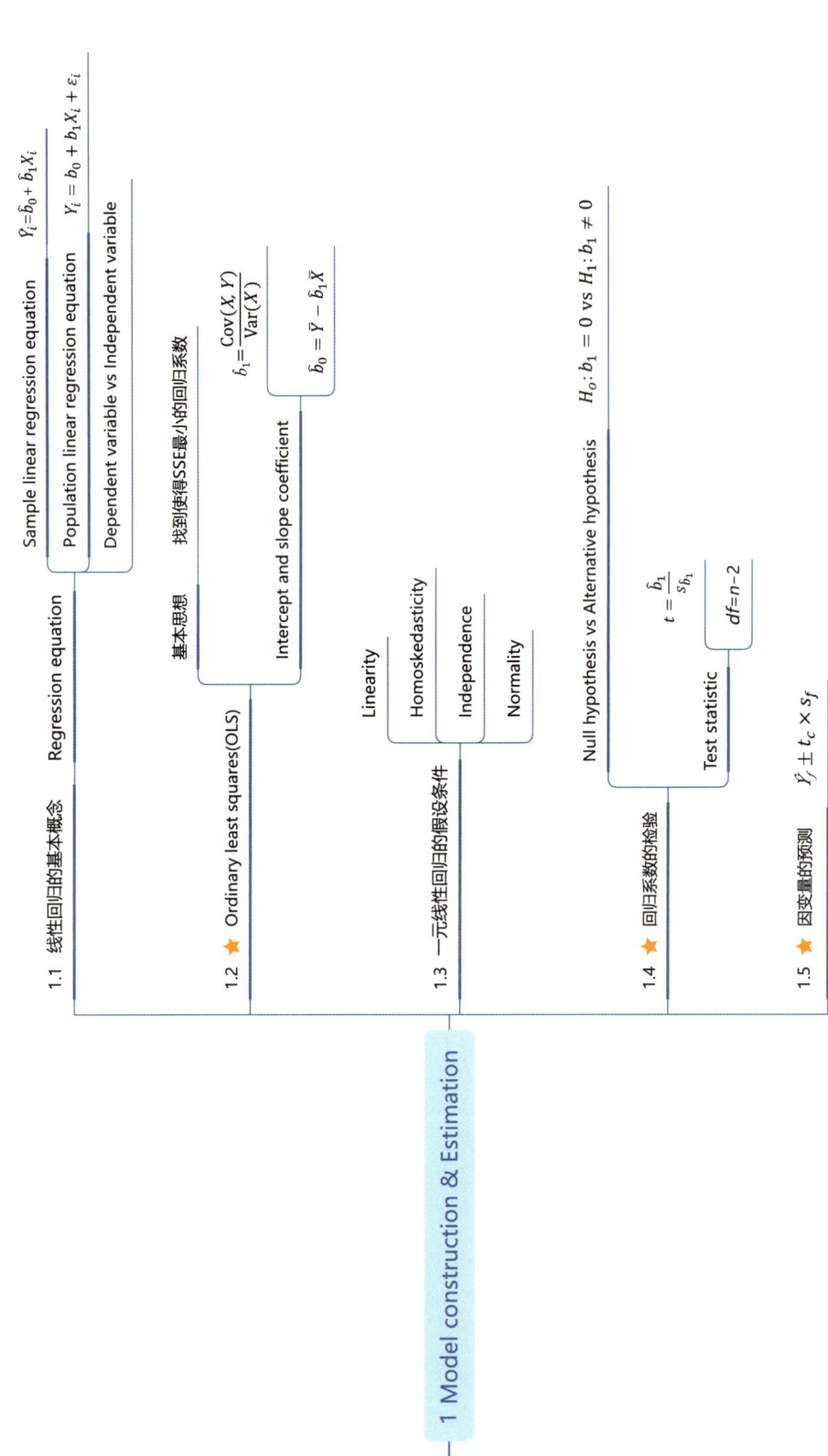

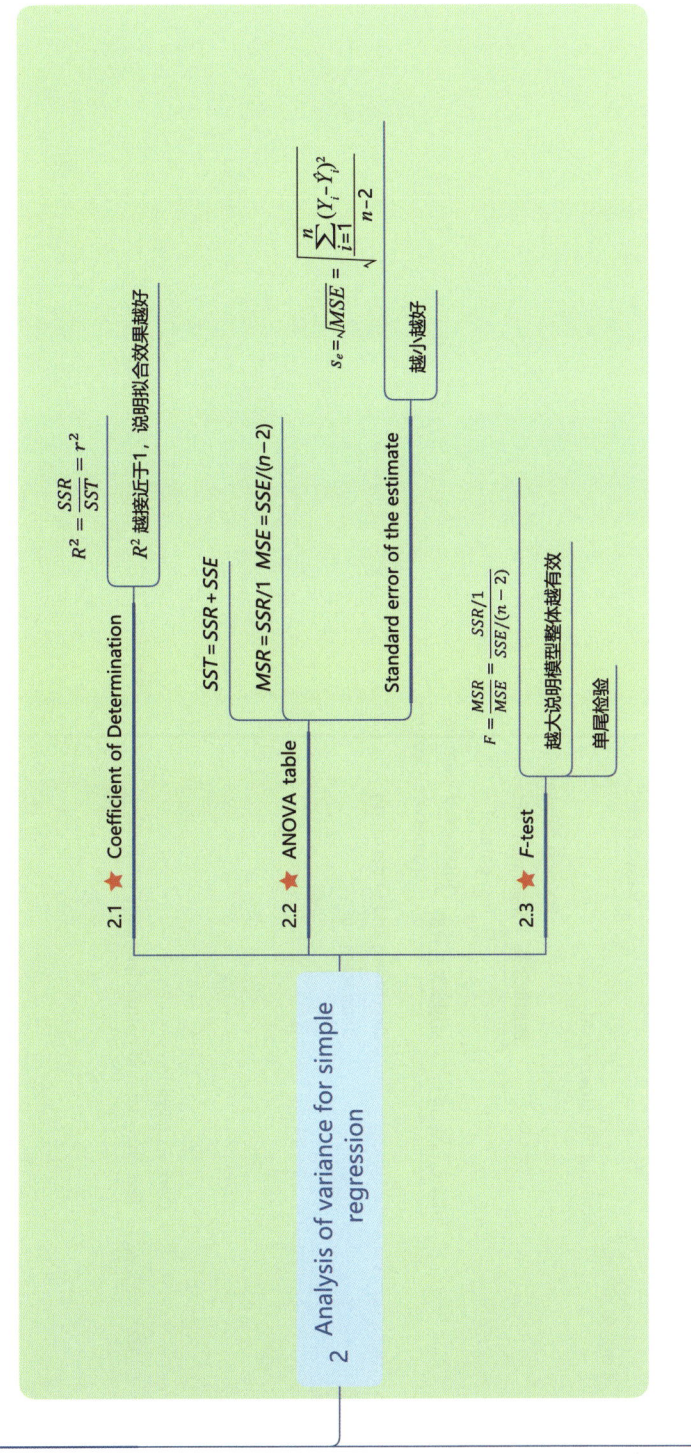

Reading 8　Introduction to Big Data Techniques

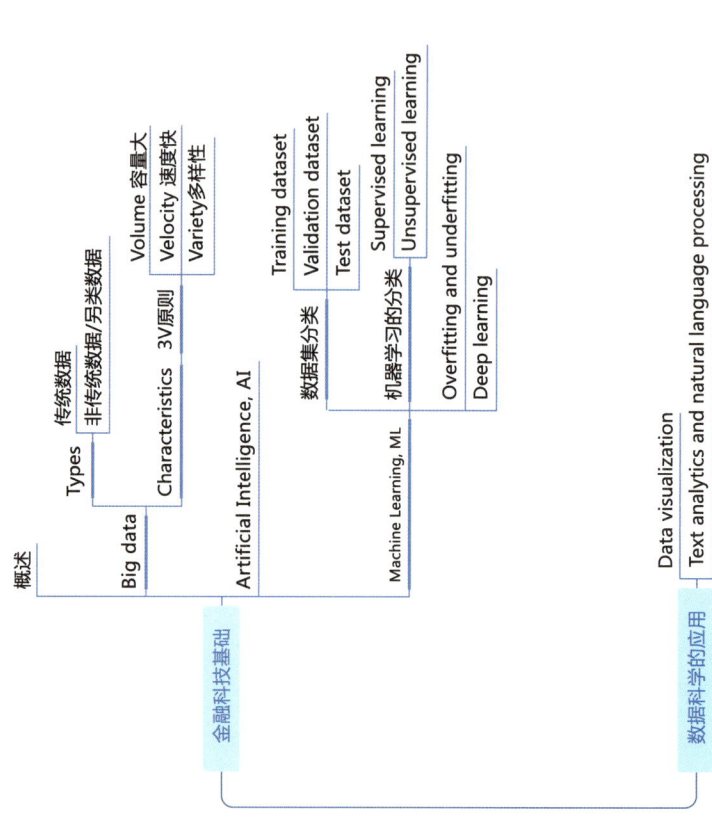

第二部分 经济学

Reading 9　Firm and Market Structures

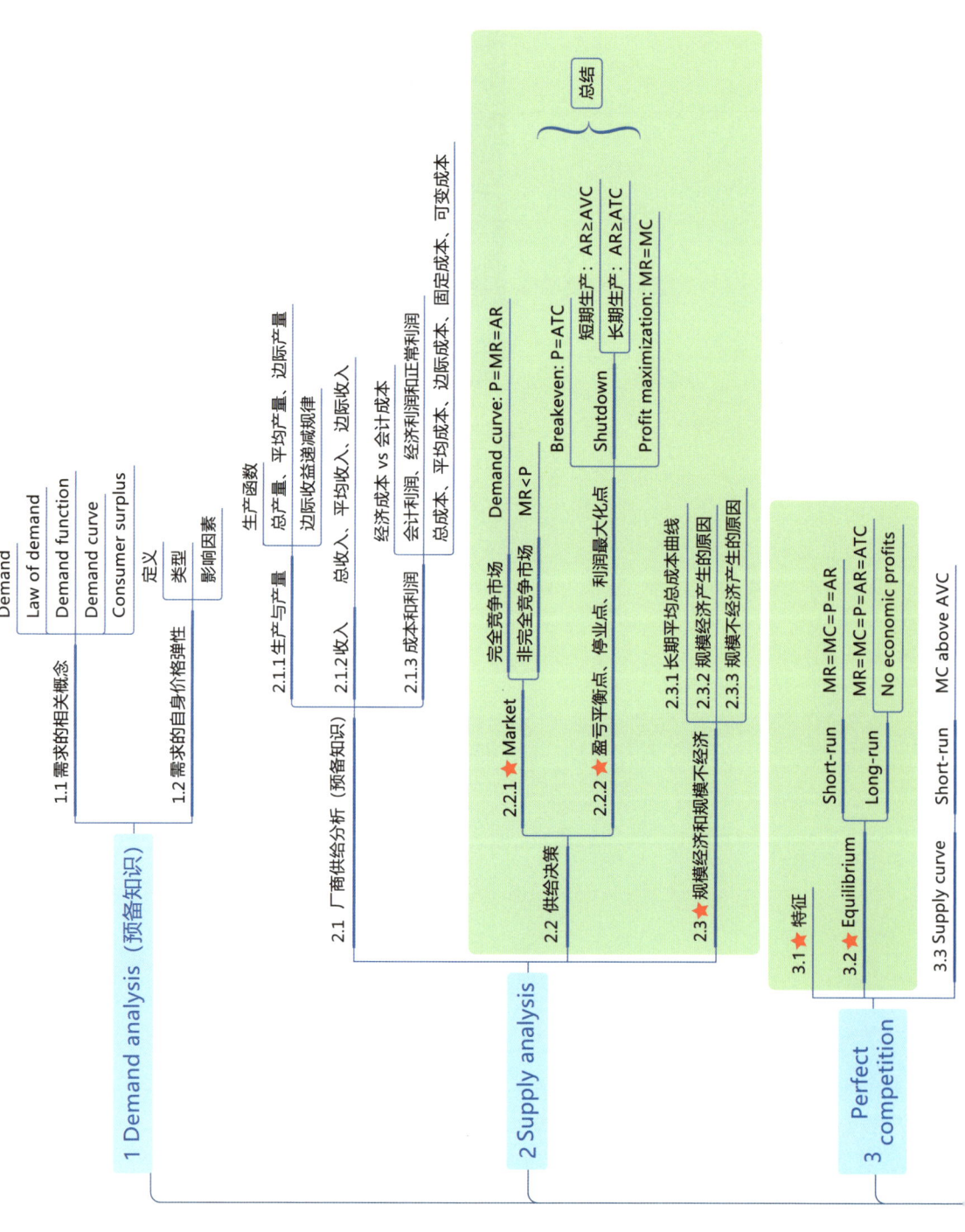

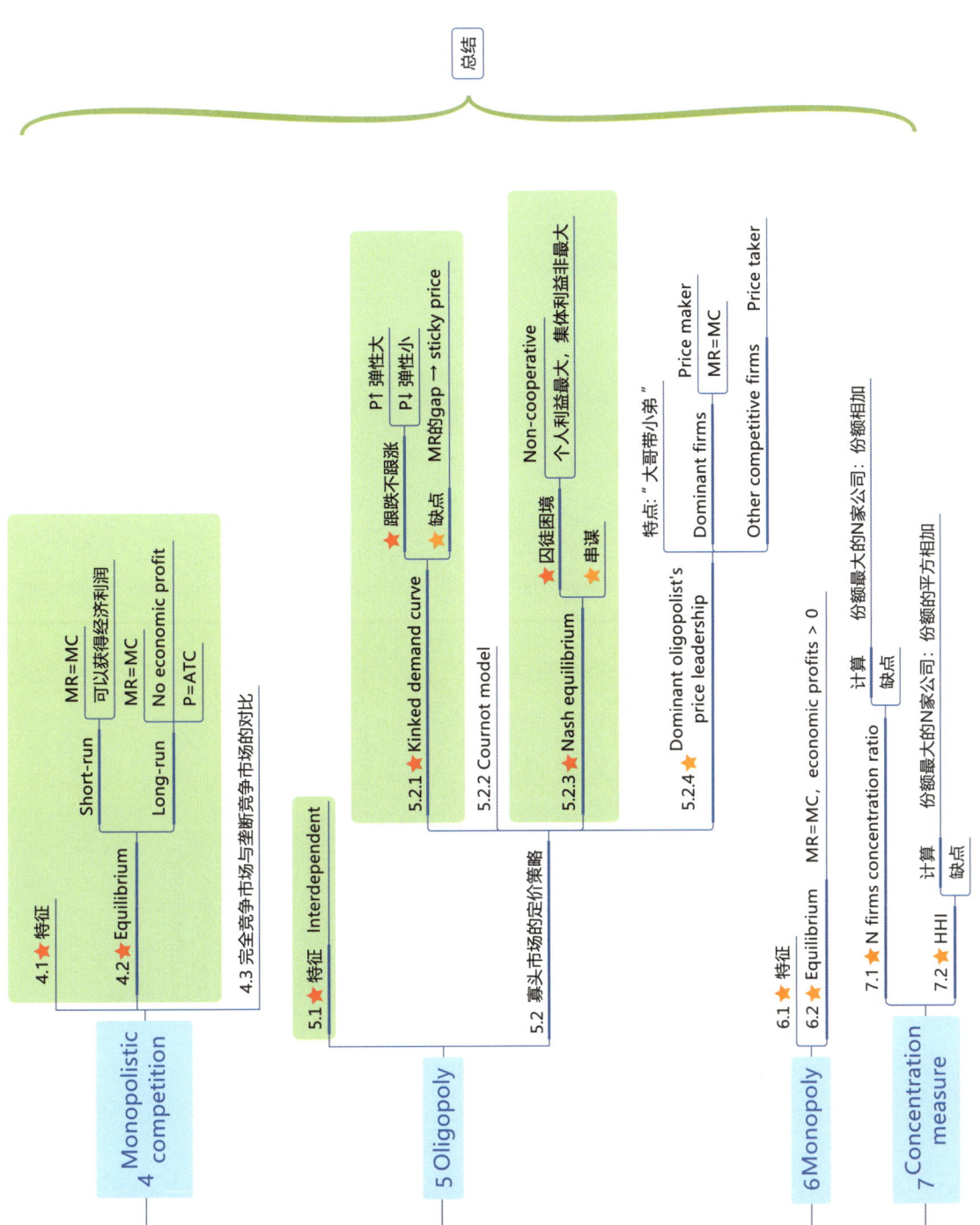

Reading 10 Understanding Business Cycles

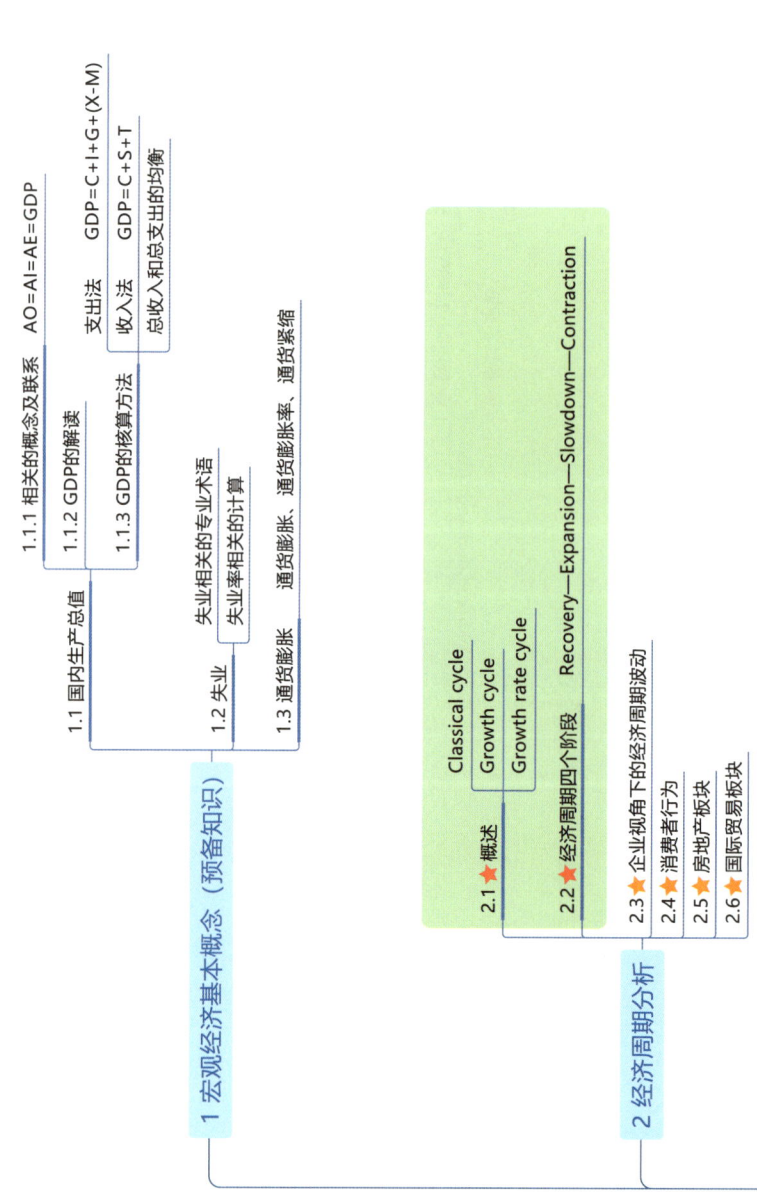

3 信贷周期

- 3.1 描述信贷周期

4 经济指标

- 4.1 ★ 经济指标的分类
  - Leading economic indicators — 预测未来
  - Coincident economic indicators — 确认现在
  - Lagging economic indicators — 确认过去
- 4.2 其他经济指标
  - 综合指数
  - 大数据的运用

Reading 11　Fiscal and Monetary Policy

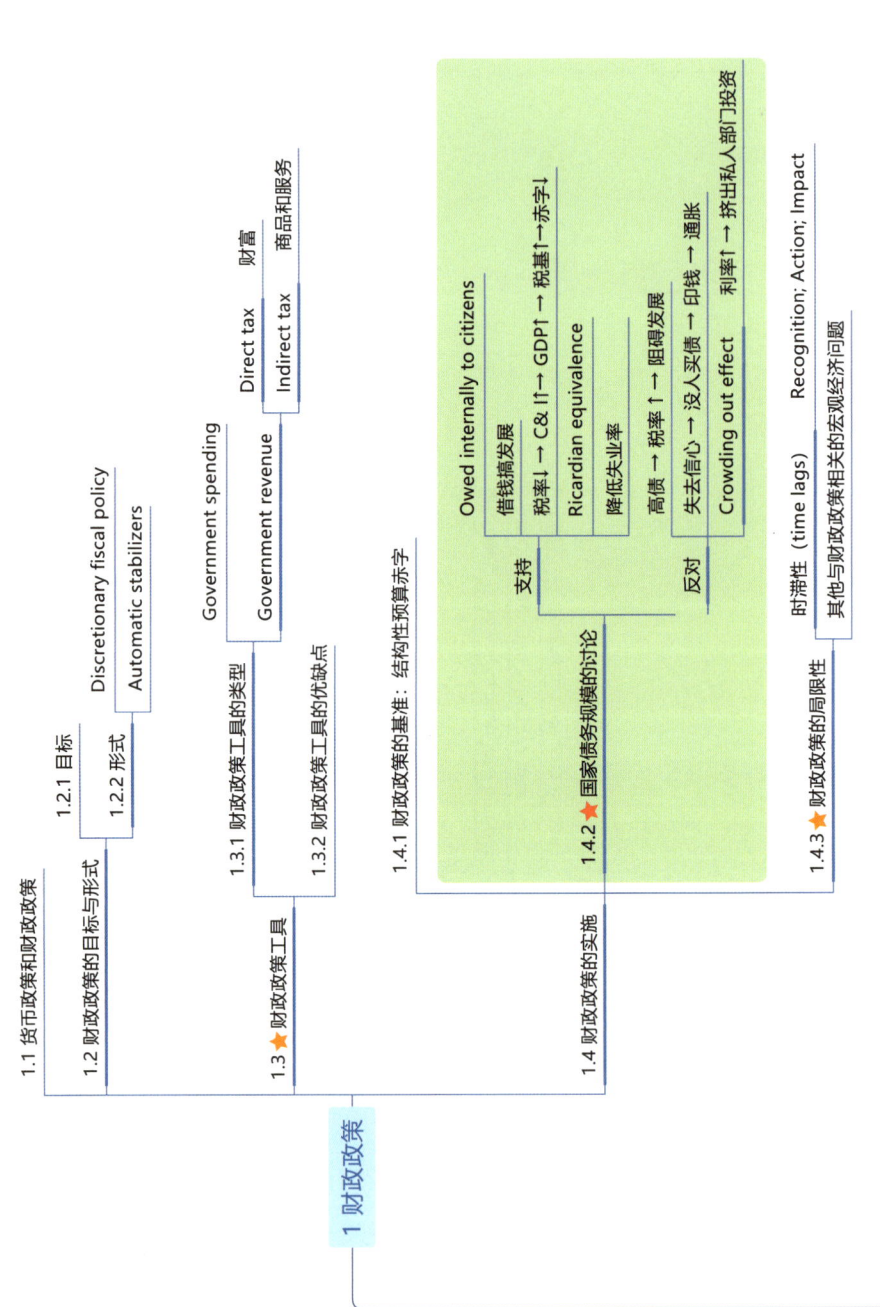

2 货币政策

- **2.1 中央银行**
  - 2.1.1 中央银行的职能
  - 2.1.2 中央银行的目标
  - 2.1.3 中央银行的有效性 —— 独立性、可信度、透明度
- **2.2 ★ 货币政策工具** —— 公开市场操作 —— Sell securities → MS↓
  - 政策利率 —— Policy rate↑ → MS↓
  - 准备金要求 —— RR↑ → MS↓
- **2.3 ★ 货币政策传导机制** —— 途径 × 4
- **2.4 货币政策的目标与形式**
  - 2.4.1 货币政策的形式 —— MS↑: Expansionary/Easy
    - MS↓: Contractionary/Tight
  - 2.4.2 ★ 货币政策的目标 —— Interest rate targeting
    - Inflation targeting
    - Exchange rate targeting
- **2.5 ★ 货币政策的实施**
  - 2.5.1 货币政策的基准：中性利率
  - 2.5.2 货币政策的局限性 —— Bond market vigilantes: 利率长短期反向
    - Liquidity trap 解决方法：QE
- **2.6 ★ 货币政策和财政政策组合**

Reading 12　International Trade

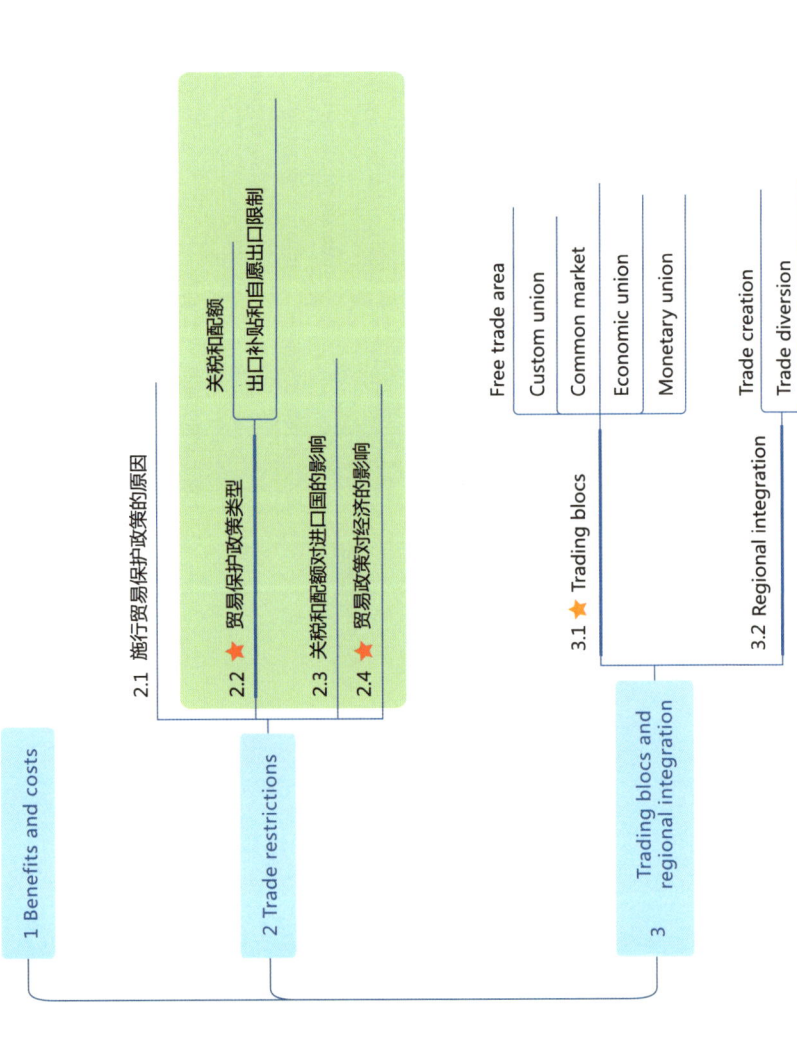

Reading 13 Capital Flows and the FX Market

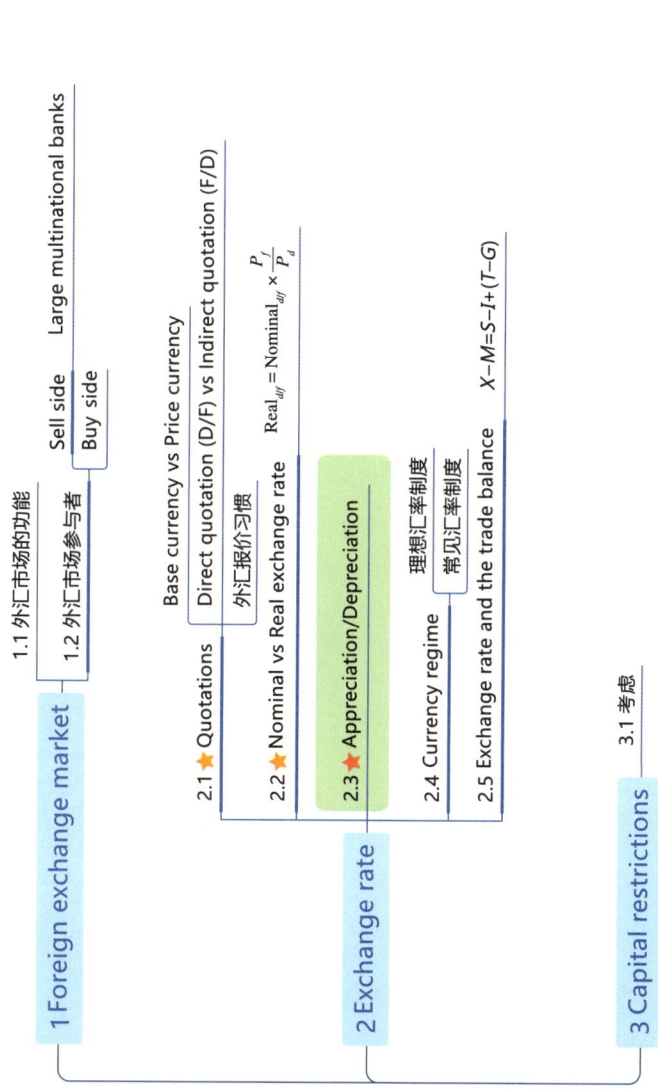

Reading 14 Exchange Rate Calculations

1 Cross-rate calculations
- 1.1 ⭐ Calculation 中间货币作为桥梁

2 Forward rate calculations
- 2.1 ⭐ Spot vs Forward exchange rate
- 2.2 Forward premium vs Forward discount
- 2.3 远期汇率报价
  - 2.3.1 Forward rate = Spot rate + 0.0001 × points
  - 2.3.2 Forward rate = Spot rate × (1 + %change)
- 2.4 ⭐ Interest rate parity (IRP)
  - 公式推导和应用
    $$F_{d/f} = S_{d/f} \times \left(\frac{1 + r_d \times \frac{Actual}{360}}{1 + r_f \times \frac{Actual}{360}} \right)$$
  - 无风险套利机会的辨别
  - 升水/贴水的计算
    $$\frac{F_{d/f} - S_{d/f}}{F_{d/f}} = \frac{r_d - r_f}{1 + r_f} \approx r_d - r_f$$

Reading 15　Introduction to Geopolitics

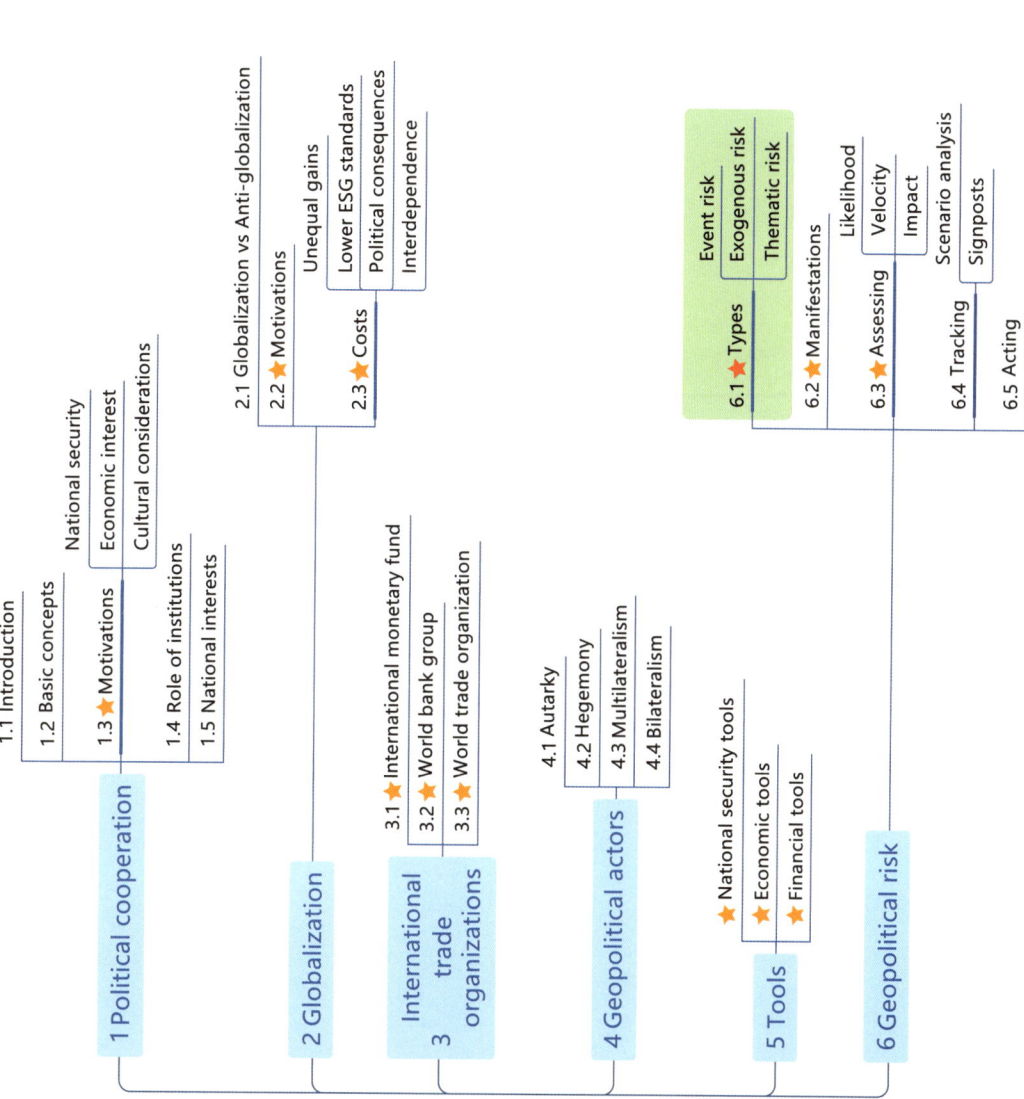

- **1 Political cooperation**
  - 1.1 Introduction
  - 1.2 Basic concepts
  - 1.3 ★ Motivations
    - National security
    - Economic interest
    - Cultural considerations
  - 1.4 Role of institutions
  - 1.5 National interests

- **2 Globalization**
  - 2.1 Globalization vs Anti-globalization
  - 2.2 ★ Motivations
  - 2.3 ★ Costs
    - Unequal gains
    - Lower ESG standards
    - Political consequences
    - Interdependence

- **3 International trade organizations**
  - 3.1 ★ International monetary fund
  - 3.2 ★ World bank group
  - 3.3 ★ World trade organization

- **4 Geopolitical actors**
  - 4.1 Autarky
  - 4.2 Hegemony
  - 4.3 Multilateralism
  - 4.4 Bilateralism

- **5 Tools**
  - ★ National security tools
  - ★ Economic tools
  - ★ Financial tools

- **6 Geopolitical risk**
  - 6.1 ★ Types
    - Event risk
    - Exogenous risk
    - Thematic risk
  - 6.2 ★ Manifestations
  - 6.3 ★ Assessing
    - Likelihood
    - Velocity
    - Impact
    - Scenario analysis
    - Signposts
  - 6.4 Tracking
  - 6.5 Acting

第三部分 财务报表分析

Reading 16　Introduction to Financial Statement Analysis

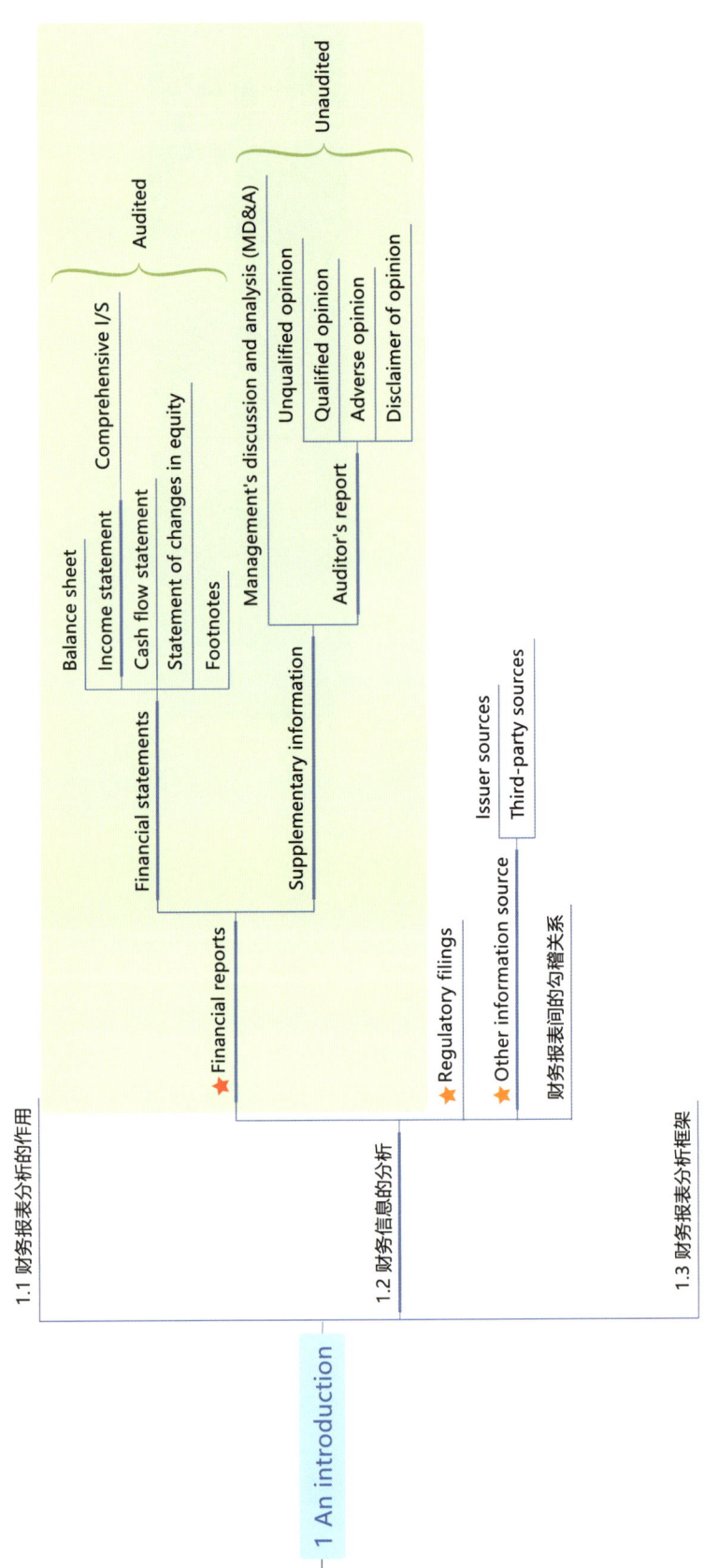

2 Financial reporting standards

- **2.1 财务报告准则制定主体和监管机构**
  - Standard-setting bodies（预备知识）
    - 国际会计准则理事会（IASB）
    - 美国财务会计准则委员会（FASB）
  - Regulatory authorities
    - 美国证券交易委员会（SEC）
    - 欧洲监管组织
      - 欧洲证券委员会（ESC）
      - 欧洲证券和市场管理局（ESMA）
    - 国际证监会组织（IOSCO）
- **2.2 国际财务报告准则框架（预备知识）**
  - Qualitative characteristics
  - Constraints
  - Underlying assumptions
- **2.3 比较财务报告体系**

Reading 17　Analyzing Income Statements

1　Components & Format
- 1.1 Elements（预备知识）
- 1.2 Format（预备知识）
- 1.3 Operating and non-operating items（预备知识）
- 1.4 Non-recurring items
  - 1.4.1 ★ Discontinued operations (below the line, after tax)
  - 1.4.2 ★ Unusual or infrequent items (above the line, before tax)
  - 1.4.3 会计变更
    - Change in accounting policies — Retrospective
    - Change in accounting estimate — Prospective
    - Correction of an error — Restatement
- 1.5 Comprehensive income（预备知识）

2　Revenue and expense recognition
- 2.1 ★ Revenue recognition
  - 2.1.1 Accrual method
  - 2.1.2 5 steps
  - 2.1.3 收入确认准则的具体运用
    - Contracts
      - Performance obligation
      - Transaction price
      - Allocation price
      - When performance obligation is satisfied
    - Long-term contract (more than one year)
    - Principal vs Agent
    - Franchising/ Licensing
    - Software as service/ License
    - Bill and hold arrangements
- 2.2 ★ Expense recognition
  - General principle: Accrual accounting and matching principle
  - 费用确认准则的具体运用
  - 财务报表分析关注的要点

3 ★ EPS

- 3.1 Simple and Complex capital structure
- 3.2 Basic EPS
  - 3.2.1 ★ 公式与计算 — 加权平均数调整
    - New issue ⎱
    - Repurchase ⎰ Weighted by time
    - Stock dividend ⎱ Not weighted by time
    - Stock split ⎰
- 3.3 Diluted EPS
  - 3.3.1 ★ 公式与计算
    - Stock options ⎫
    - Warrants ⎬ Potential dilutive financial instruments
    - Convertible debt ⎪
    - Convertible preferred stock ⎭

4 Analysis of income statement

- Common-size I/S
- Percentage of net revenue

Reading 18　Analyzing Balance Sheets

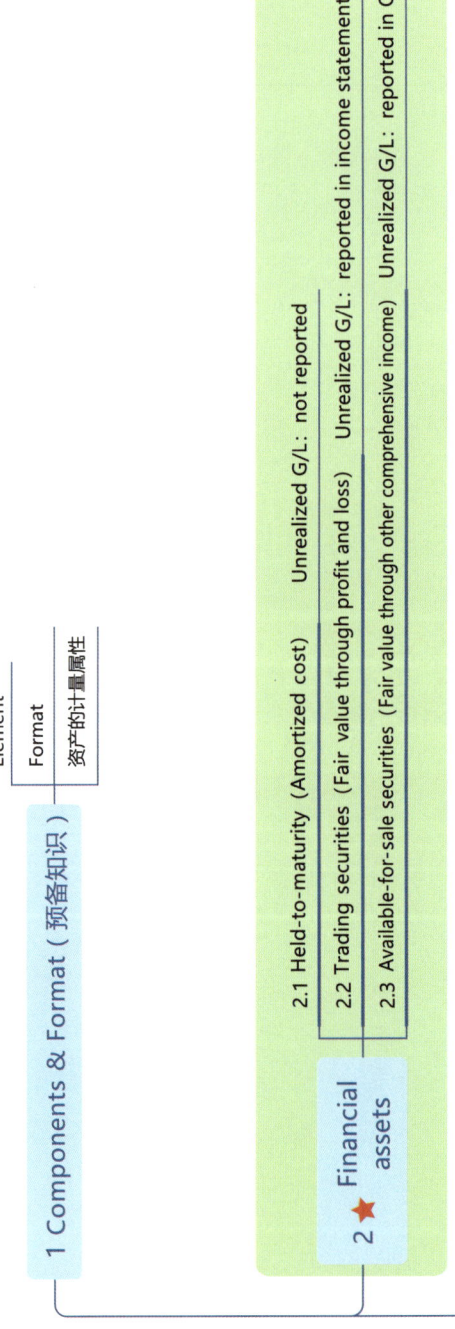

Reading 19 Analyzing Statements of Cash Flows

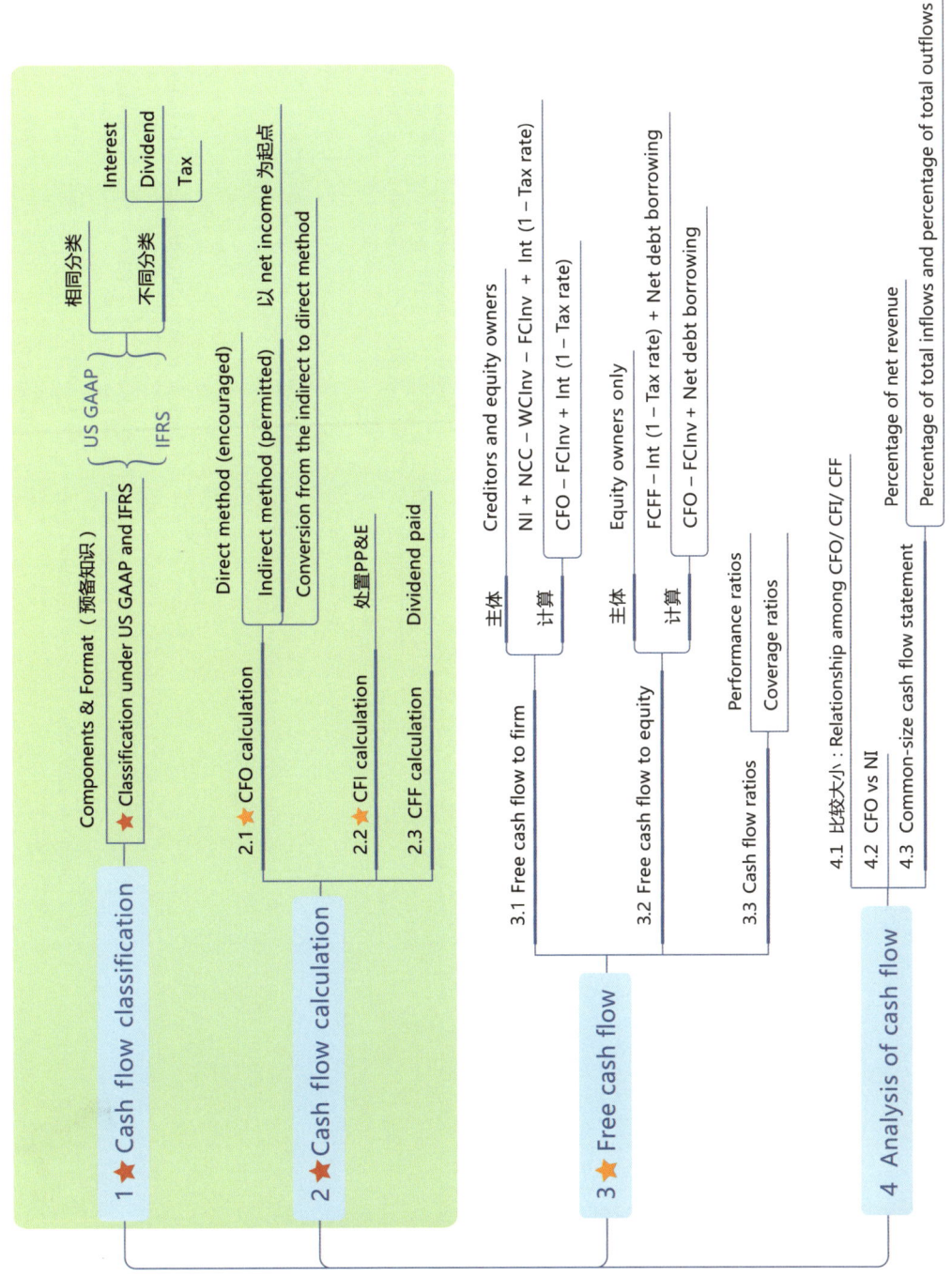

Reading 20 Financial Analysis Techniques

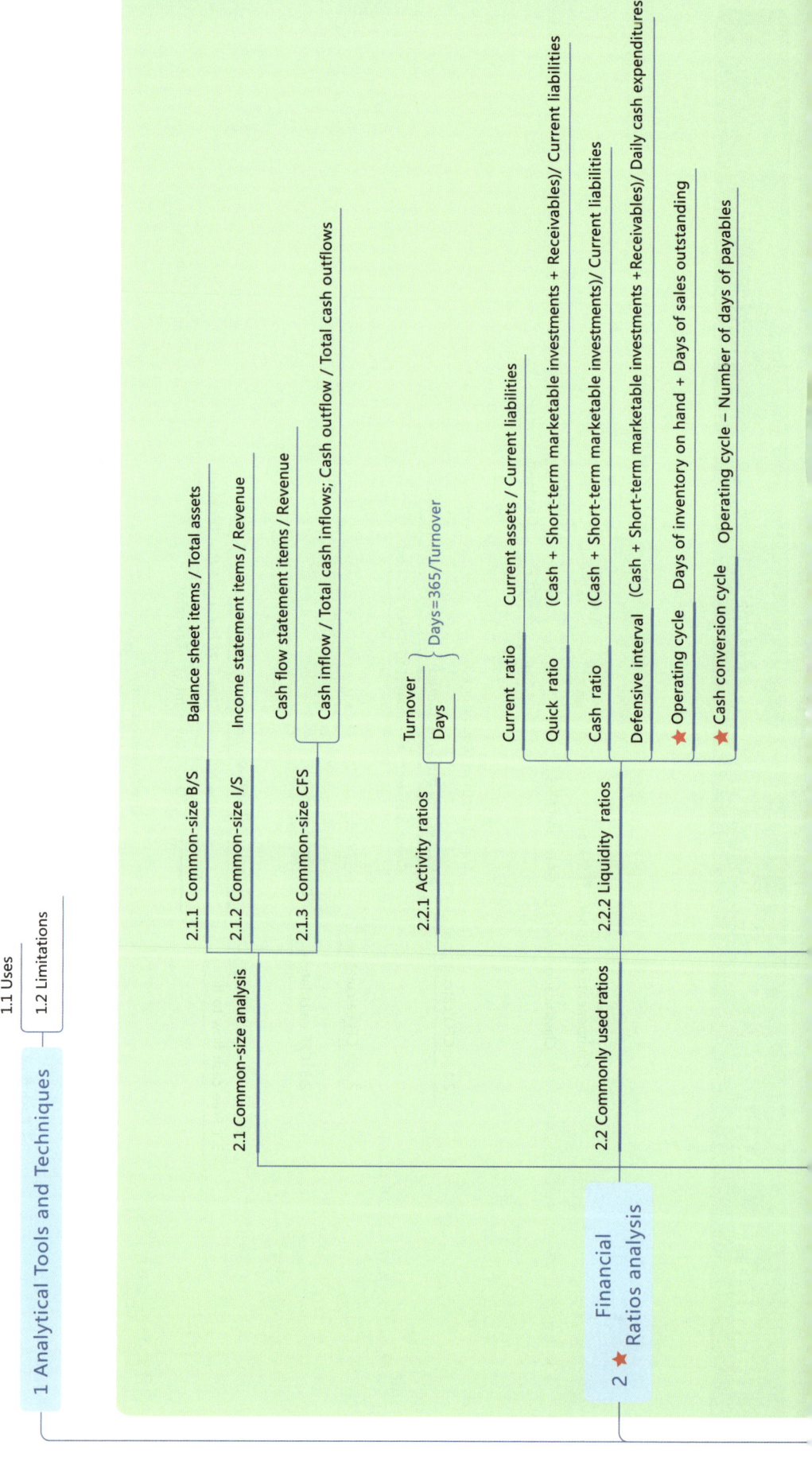

- 2.2.3 Solvency ratios
  - Debt-to-equity ratio — Total debt / Total shareholder's equity
  - Debt-to-assets ratio — Total debt / Total assets
  - Financial leverage — Average total assets / Average total equity
  - ⭐ Interest coverage — EBIT / Interest
  - ⭐ Fixed charge coverage — (EBIT + Lease payments) / (Interest + Lease payments)

- 2.2.4 Profitability ratios
  - 2.2.4.1 Return on sales
    - Gross profit margin — Gross profit / Net revenue
    - Operating profit margin — Operating income / Net revenue
    - Pretax margin — EBT / Net revenue
    - Net profit margin — Net income / Net revenue
  - 2.2.4.2 Return on investment
    - ROA
      - NI / Average total assets (definition)
      - [NI + Int(1 − Tax rate)] / Average total assets (for analysis)
    - Return on capital — EBIT(1 − t) / Average debt & equity
    - ROE — NI / Average total equity

- 2.3 Industry-specific ratios

- 2.4 Model building and forecasting
  - Sensitivity analysis
  - Scenario analysis
  - Simulation

3 DuPont analysis
- 3.1 Three-step analysis
- 3.2 Five-step analysis

Reading 21　Analysis of Inventories

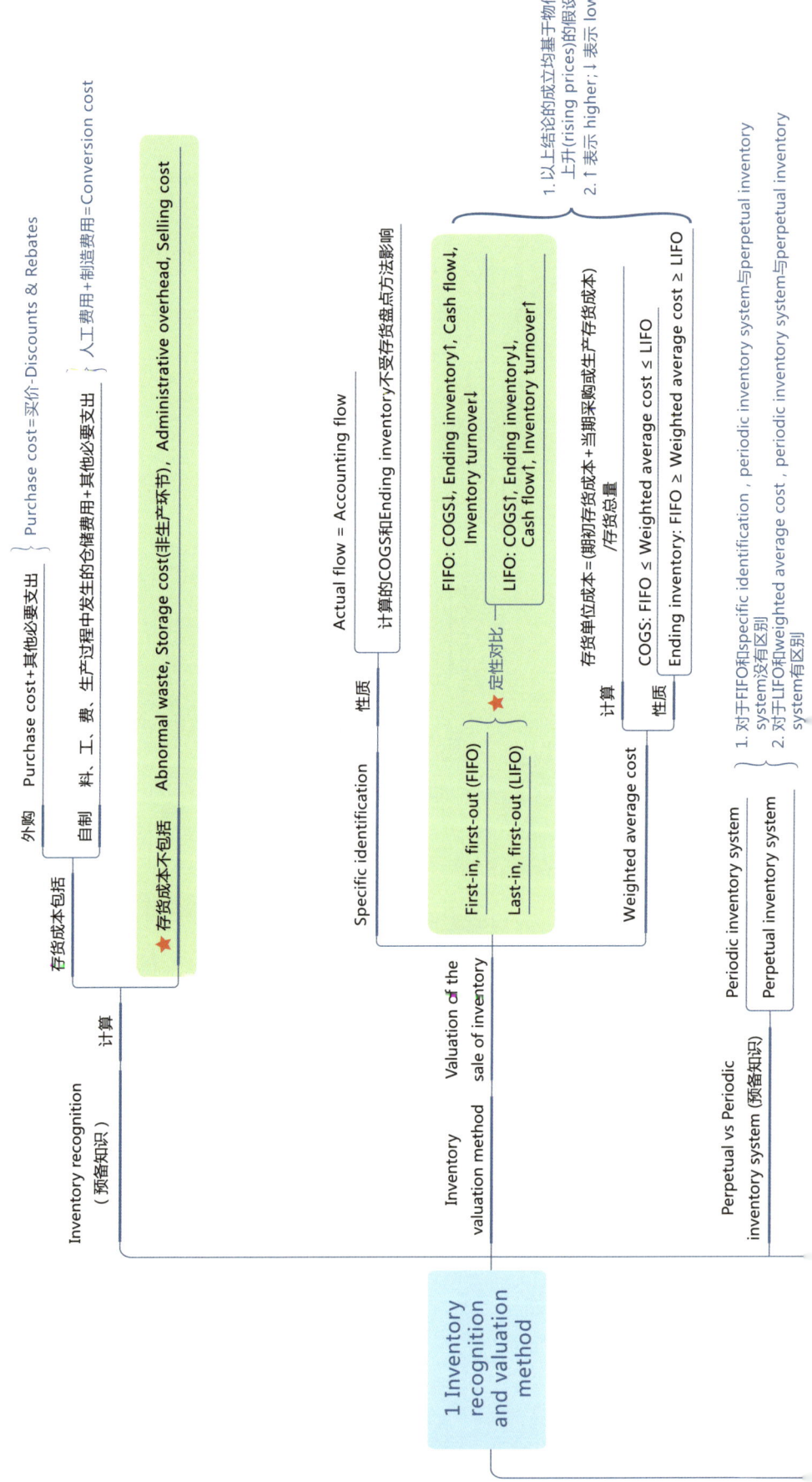

LIFO reserve and LIFO liquidation（预备知识）

LIFO reserve

定义: 报表中披露的用于将LIFO下的存货数据调整为FIFO下的对应存货数据的科目，通常由使用LIFO方法的公司于财务附注中披露

计算:
- ★ B/S调整: $\text{Ending inventory}_{FIFO} = \text{Ending inventory}_{LIFO} + \text{LIFO reserve}$
- ★ I/S调整: $\text{COGS}_{FIFO} = \text{COGS}_{LIFO} - \Delta\text{LIFO reserve}$

LIFO liquidation

★ **后果**:
- COGS不能反映最新市场价格
- LIFO reserve可能下降
- 分析师需要调整LIFO liquidation对I/S的影响

2 Inventory adjustments

计算:
- IFRS: Cost-NRV, 减值金额计入COGS
- US GAAP: Cost-"Market", 减值金额计入COGS

★ **Reversals of inventory write-downs**:
- IFRS: 以original write-down 为限可以转回(Gain≤|Loss|)，转回金额令COGS下降
- US GAAP: 不允许转回

Other issues

3 Disclosures of

3.1 Changes of valuation methods

3.2 Presentation and disclosures

3.3 Analysis of inventory ratios and related financial statements

Reading 22　Analysis of Long-Term Assets

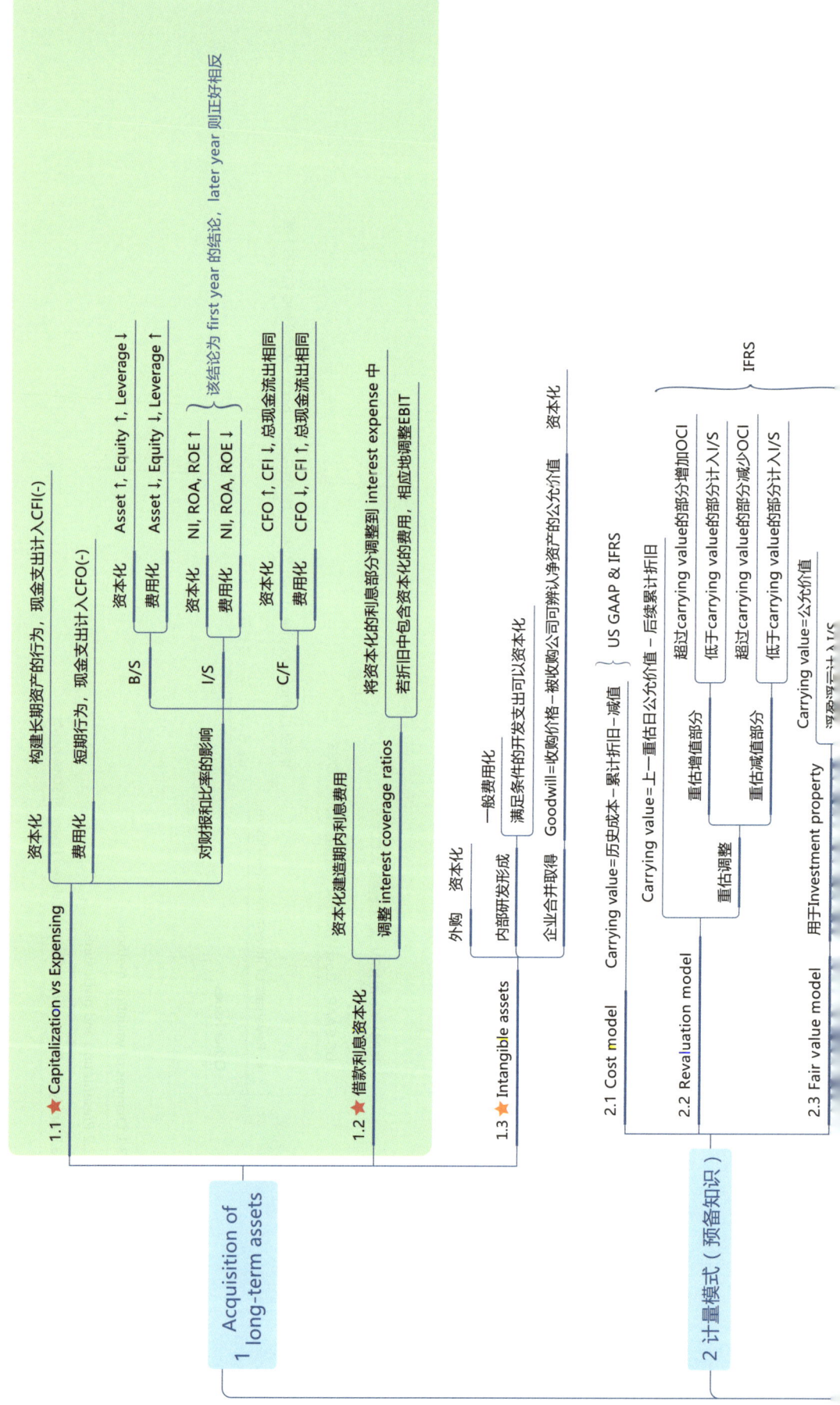

3 Depreciation method (预备知识)

3.1 计算
- Straight-line method
- DDB: 折旧 $= \dfrac{2}{\text{使用年限}} \times$ 期初账面价值
- Units of production

4 Impairment and derecognition

4.1 长期资产的减值

★ Held for use 长期资产的减值

- IFRS
  - Step 1: If Carrying value > Recoverable amount = Higher of (NRV, Value in use)
  - Step 2: Loss = Carrying value − Recoverable amount
  - 允许以减值金额为限转回
- US GAAP
  - Step 1: If Carrying value > Undiscounted future cash flows
  - Step 2: Loss = Carrying value − Fair value
  - 不允许转回

Held for sale 长期资产的减值
- If Carrying value > NRV, 下调至 NRV, 损失计入 I/S
- 可以转回 (IFRS & US GAAP)

★ 减值对财报和比率的影响
- Asset ↓
- Equity ↓
- D/E ↑
- Current income, ROA, ROE ↓
- Future depreciation expense ↓
- Future income, ROA, ROE ↑
- Future asset turnover ratios ↑
- Cash flow (same)

4.2 ★ 长期资产的终止
- 出售
- 弃置
- 交换

5 Disclosures of long-term assets

- 5.1 固定资产的披露
- 5.2 无形资产的披露
- 5.3 固定资产的分析比率
  - 固定资产周转率
  - 资产年限比率

Reading 23 Topics in Long-Term Liabilities and Equity

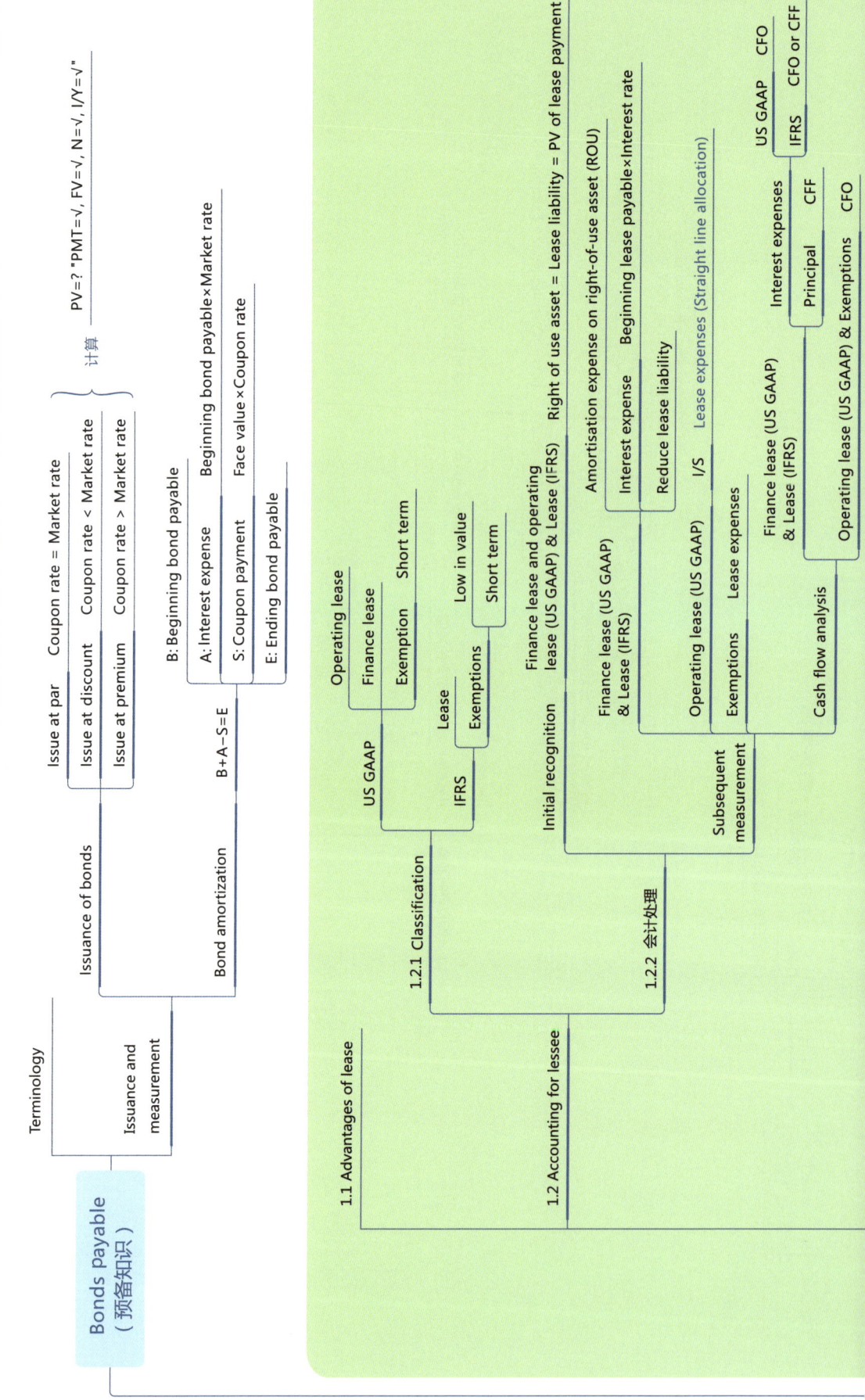

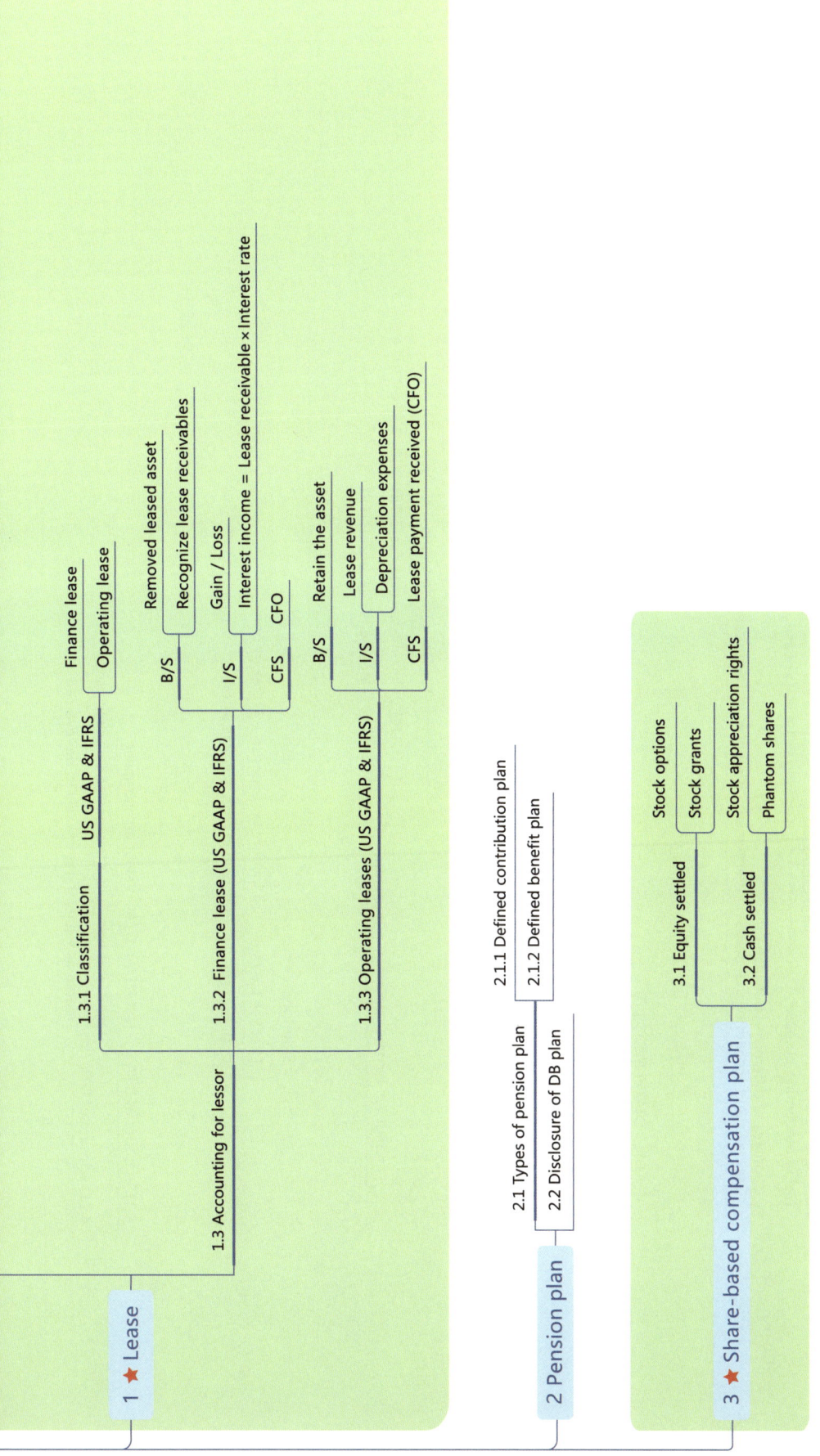

Reading 24 Analysis of Income Taxes

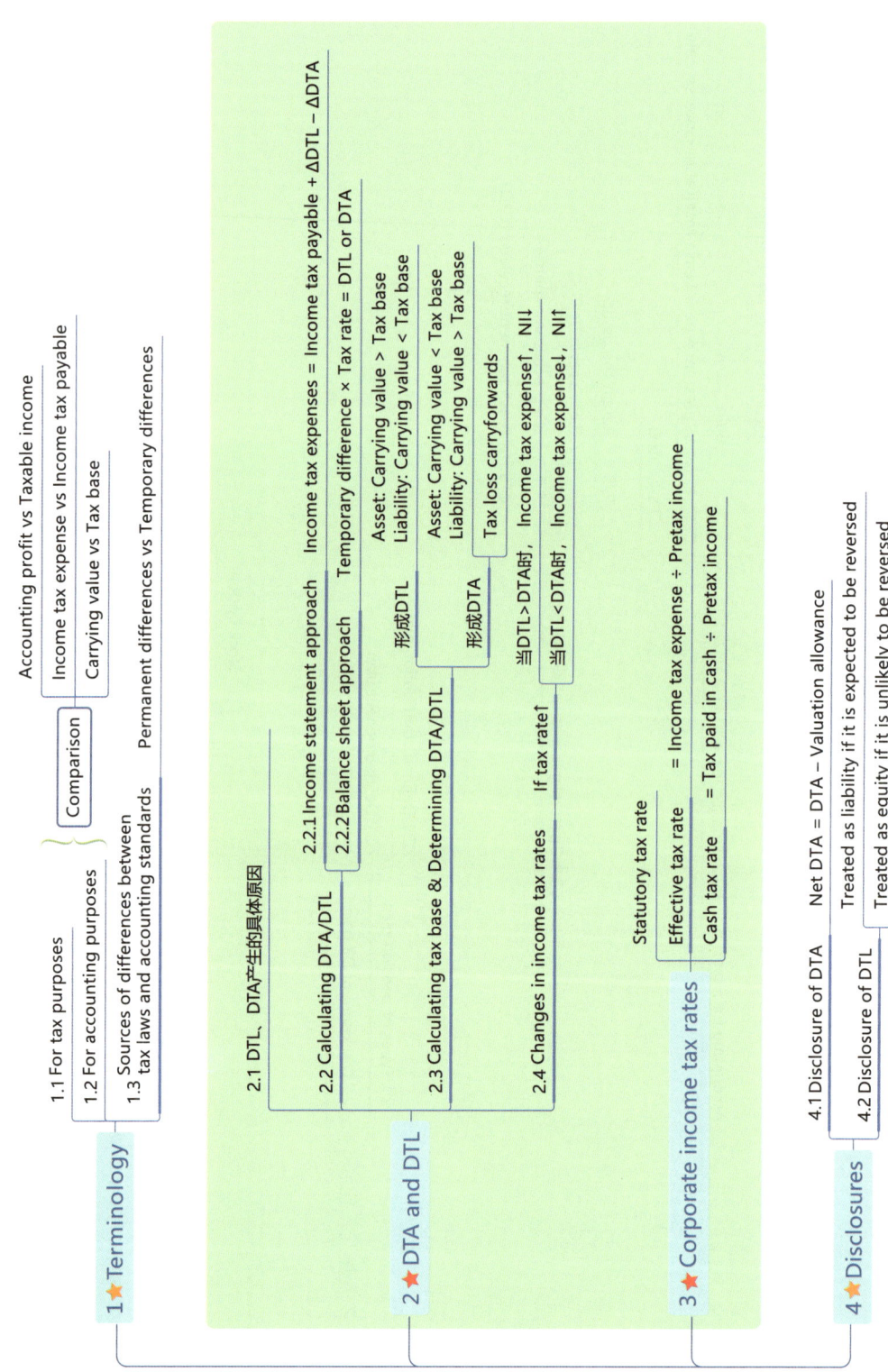

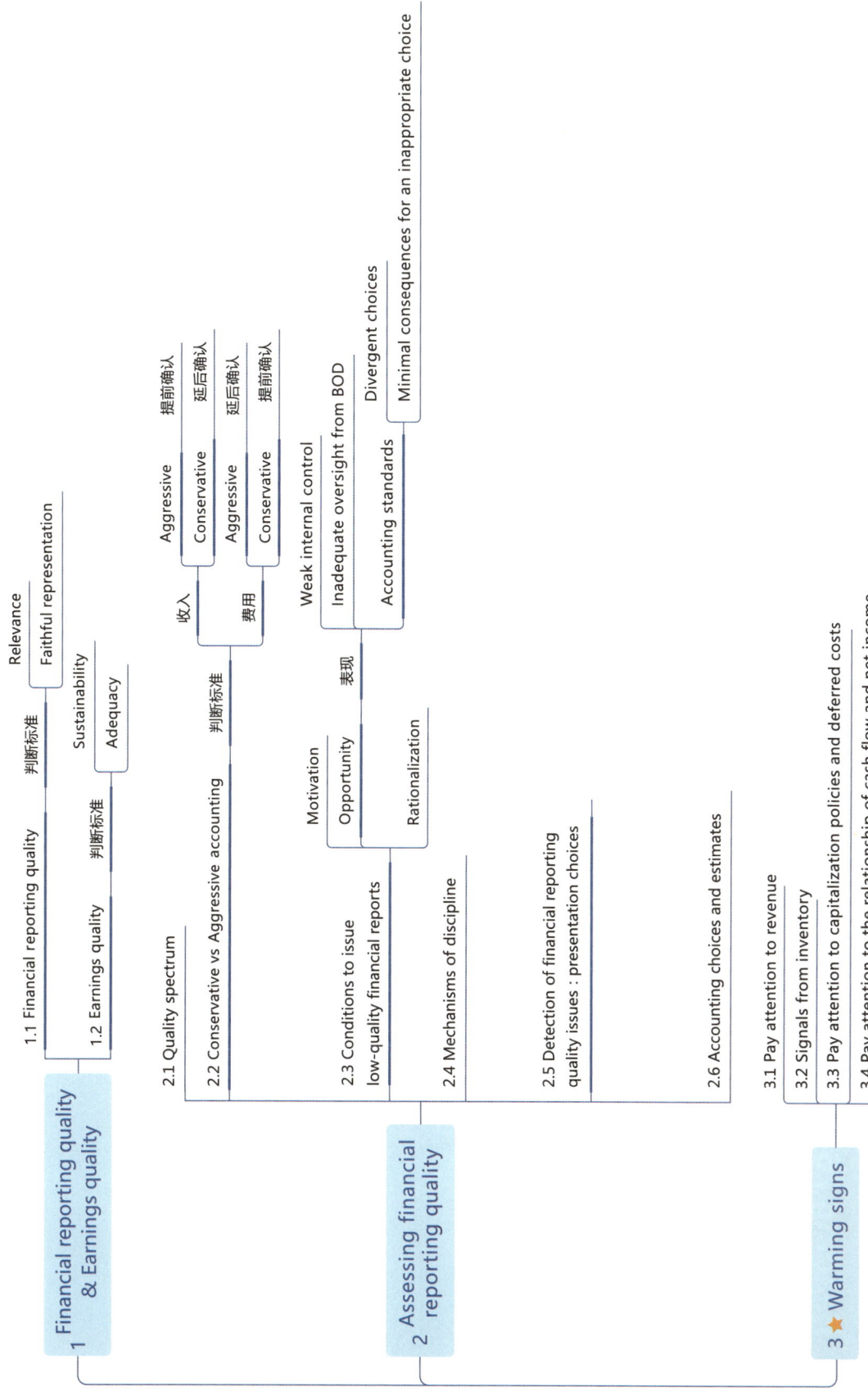

Reading 26 Introduction to Financial Statement Modeling

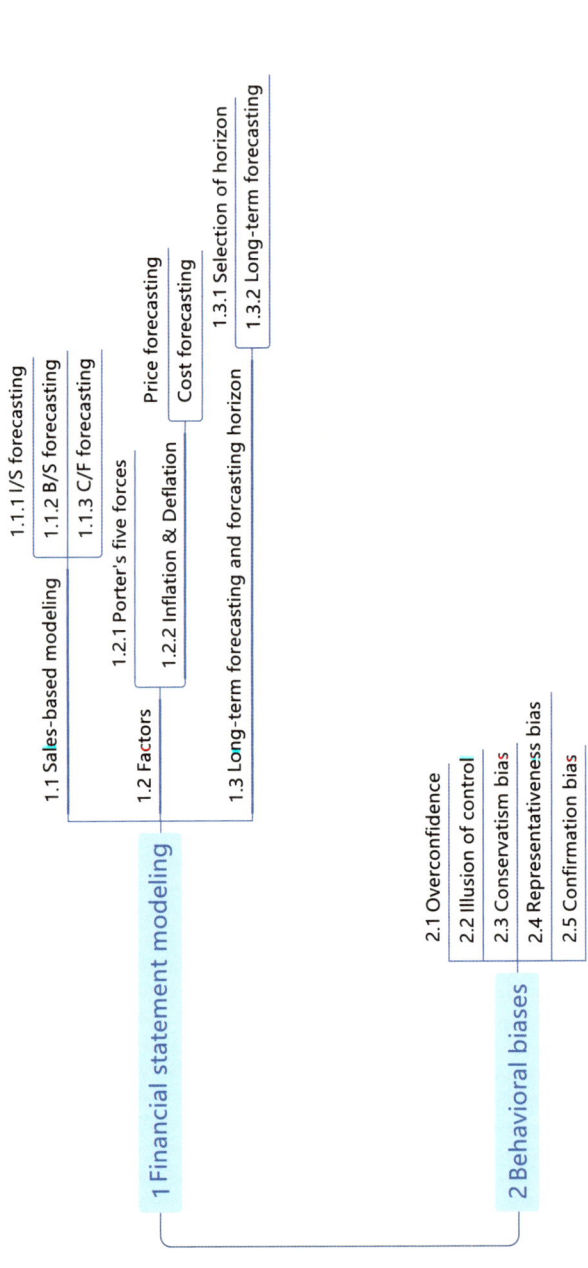

第四部分 公司发行人

Reading 27　Organizational Forms, Corporate Issuer Feature, and Ownership

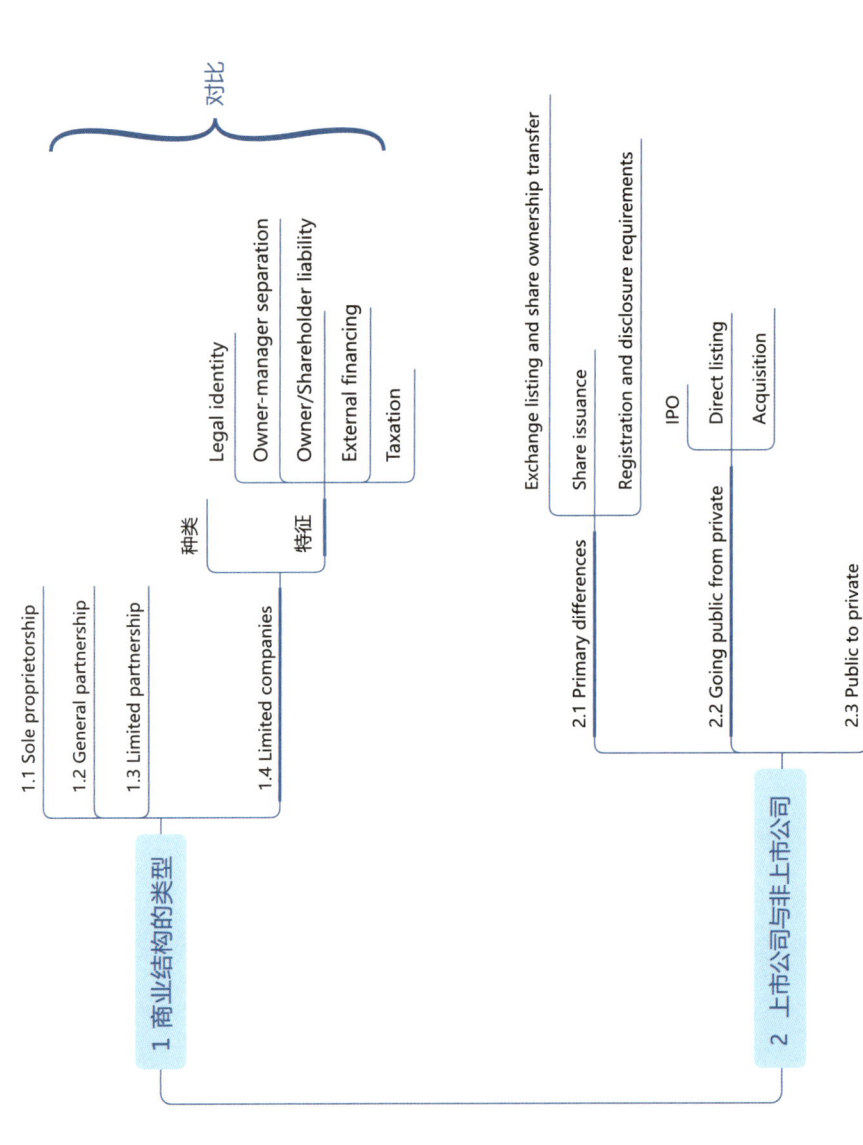

Reading 28　Investors and Other Stakeholders

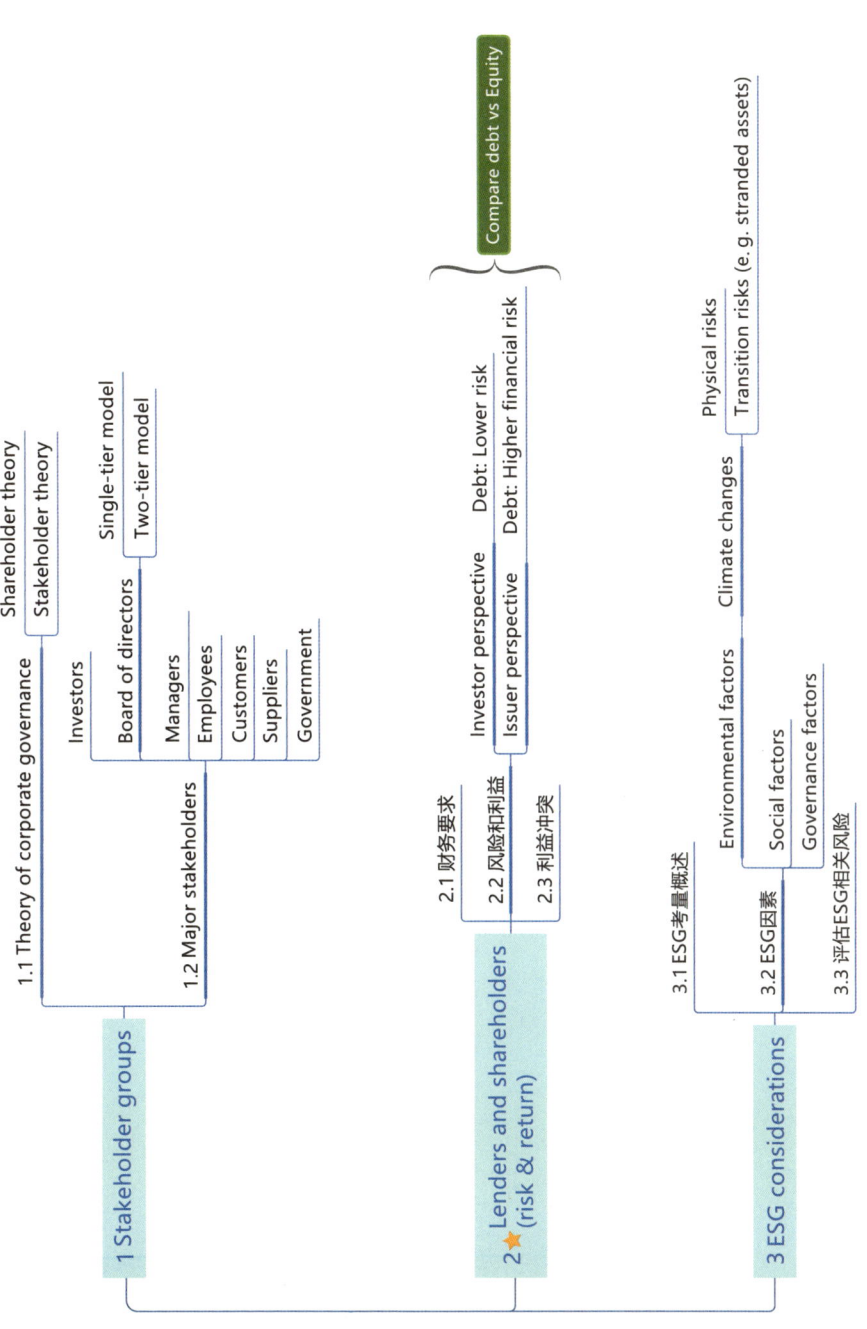

Reading 29 Corporate Governance: Conflicts, Mechanisms, Risks, and Benefits

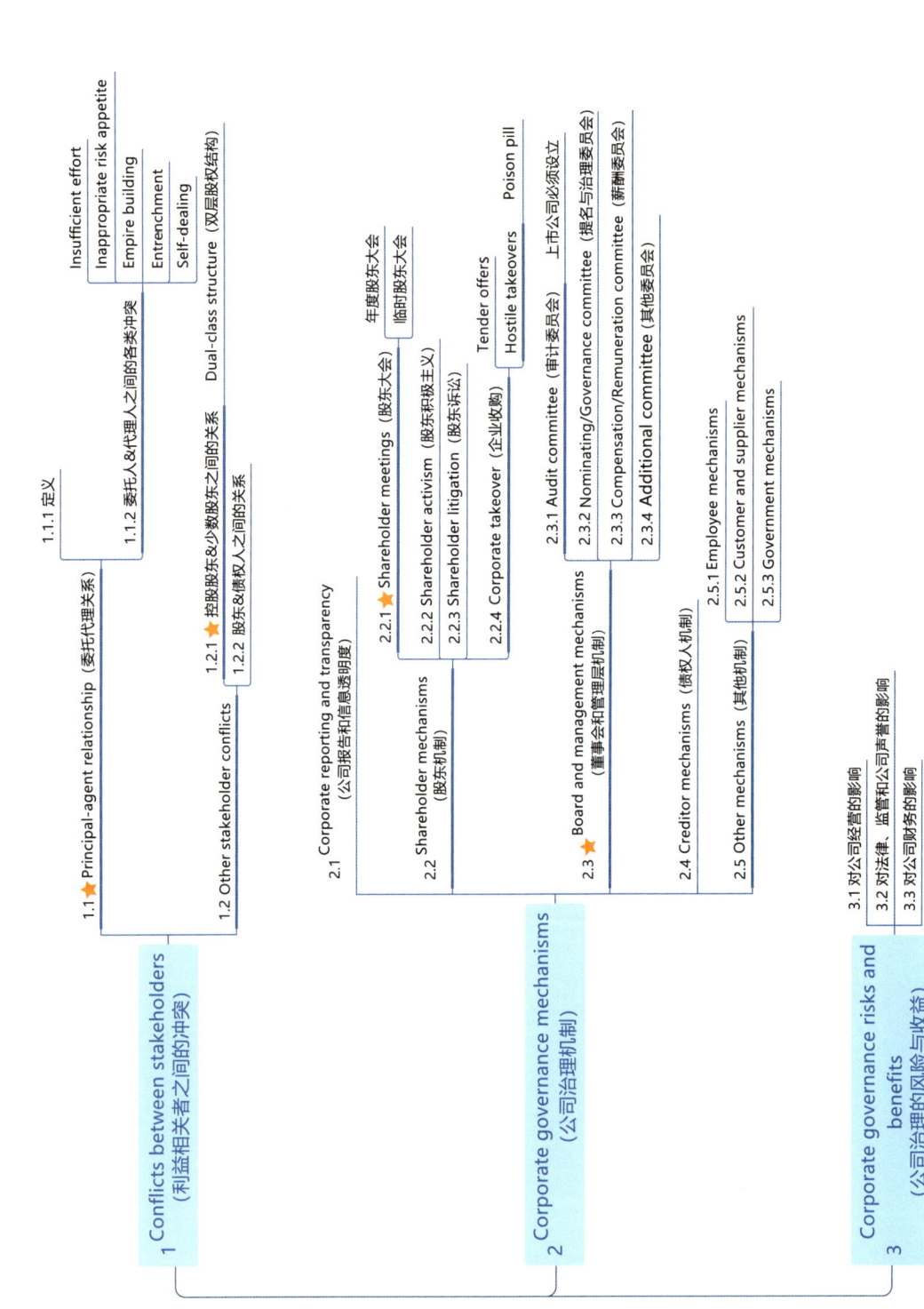

Reading 30 Business Models

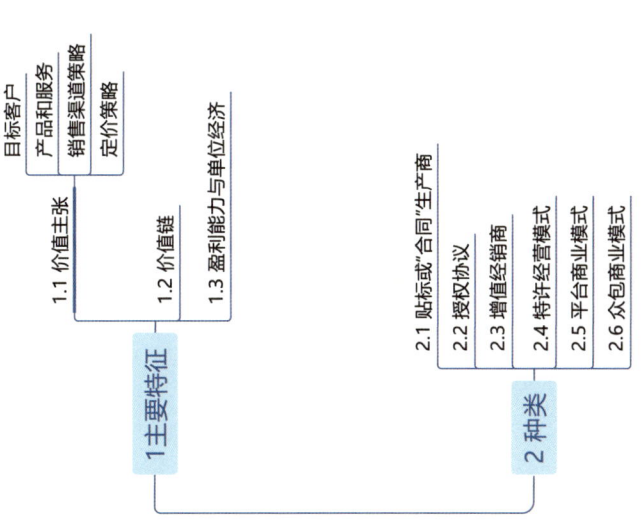

Reading 31　Working Capital & Liquidity

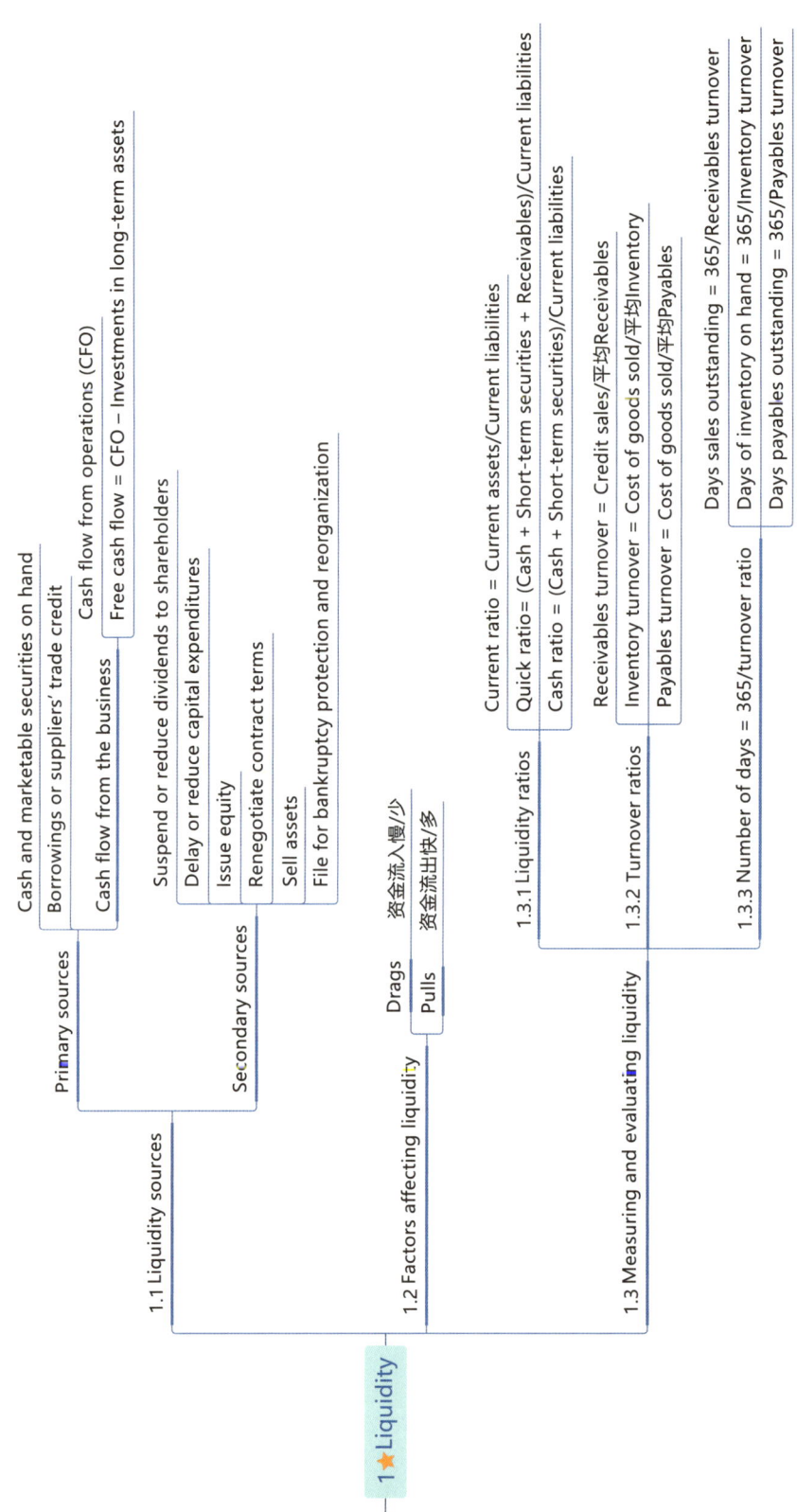

2 ★ Cash conversion cycle

- **2.1 Operating cycle**
  - 2.1.1 Operating cycle = Days sales outstanding + Days of inventory on hand
- **2.2 Cash conversion cycle**
  - 2.2.1 Cash conversion cycle = Operating cycle − Days payables outstanding
- **2.3 Internal vs External financing**
  - 2.3.1 Effective annual rate (EAR) on the trade credit = $\left(\left(1 + \frac{\text{Discount\%}}{100\% - \text{Discount\%}}\right)^{\frac{\text{Days In Year}}{\text{Payment Period} - \text{Discount Period}}}\right) - 1$

3 Working capital management

- **3.1 Definitions**
  - Total working capital = Current assets − Current liabilities
  - Net working capital = (Current assets − Cash & Marketable securities) − (Current liabilities − Short-term & Current debt)
- **3.2 ★ Management approach**
  - 3.2.1 Conservative
    - More cash, receivables and inventories
    - More reliance on long-term funding sources
  - 3.2.2 Moderate
    - Between the two approaches above
  - 3.2.3 Aggressive
    - Minimize excess cash, receivables and inventories
    - More reliance on short-term funding
- **3.3 Short-term funding**
  - Major objectives
  - Influential factors

Reading 32　Capital Investments and Capital Allocation

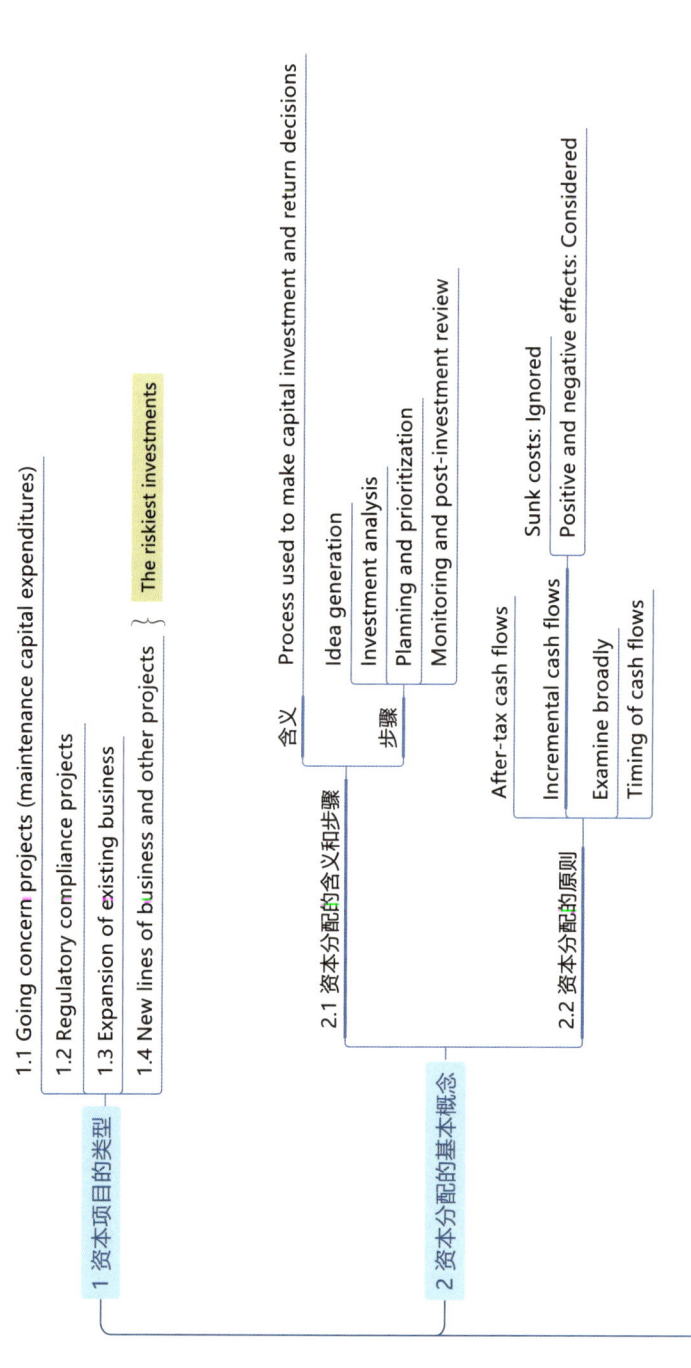

3 投资决策标准

3.1 ★ 单个项目评估方法

- 净现值法（NPV）
  - $NPV = CF_0 + \sum_{t=1}^{T} \frac{CF_t}{(1+r)^t}$
  - NPV≥0，投资；NPV<0，不投资
- 内部收益率法（IRR）
  - $\sum_{t=0}^{T} \frac{CF_t}{(1+IRR)^t} = 0$
  - IRR≥r，投资；IRR<r，不投资
  - r 是 required rate of return, 也称为 hurdle rate
- 投入资本回报率法（ROIC）
  - $ROIC = \frac{Operating\ profit \times (1 - tax\ rate)}{Average\ total\ long\text{-}term\ liabilities\ and\ equity}$
- 优点和缺点

3.2 资本分配中的常见错误
- 认知错误（Cognitive errors）
- 行为偏差（Behavioral biases）

4 实物期权

4.1 期权种类
- 择时期权（Timing option）
- 规模选择权（Sizing option）
  - Abandonment option
  - Growth option
- 灵活期权（Flexibility option）
  - Pricing-setting option
  - Production flexibility option
- 基础期权（Fundamental option）
- 含期权项目的NPV公式：NPV with options = NPV without options + Option value − Option cost

4.2 期权决策树（Decision trees）
- 概念
- 计算

Reading 33　Capital Structure

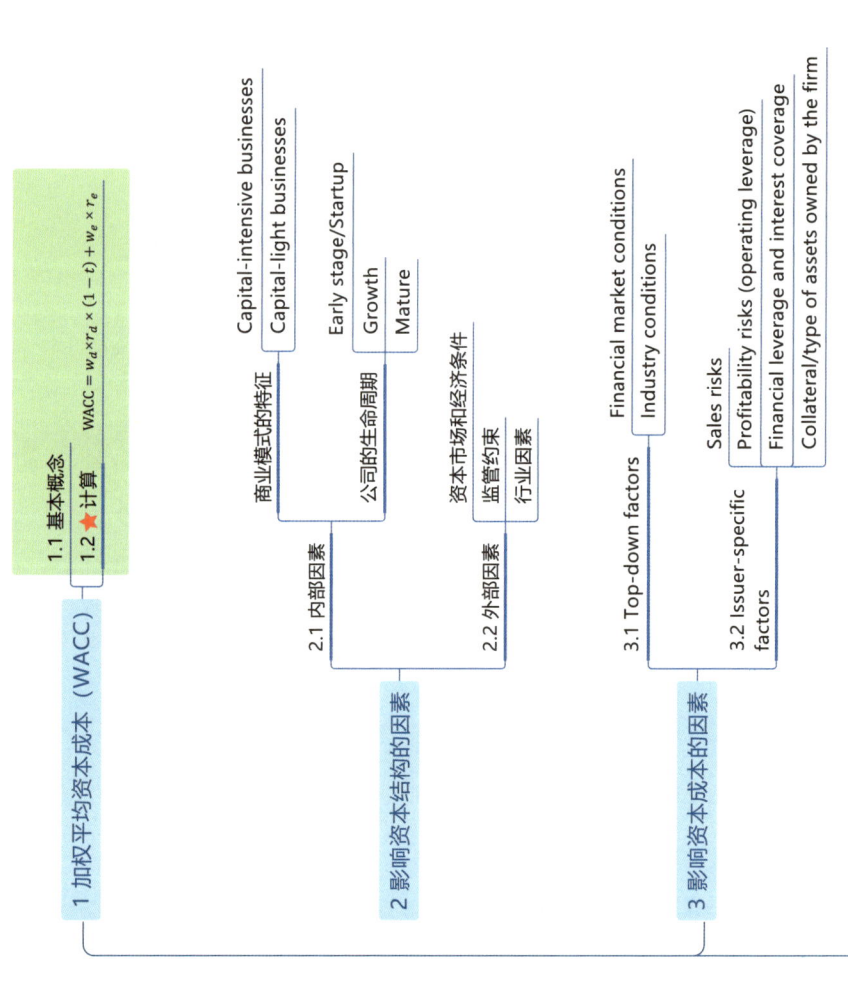

- 1 加权平均资本成本（WACC）
  - 1.1 基本概念
  - 1.2 ★ 计算　　$WACC = w_d \times r_d \times (1-t) + w_e \times r_e$
- 2 影响资本结构的因素
  - 2.1 内部因素
    - 商业模式的特征
      - Capital-intensive businesses
      - Capital-light businesses
    - 公司的生命周期
      - Early stage/Startup
      - Growth
      - Mature
  - 2.2 外部因素
    - 资本市场和经济条件
    - 监管约束
    - 行业因素
- 3 影响资本成本的因素
  - 3.1 Top-down factors
    - Financial market conditions
    - Industry conditions
  - 3.2 Issuer-specific factors
    - Sales risks
    - Profitability risks (operating leverage)
    - Financial leverage and interest coverage
    - Collateral/type of assets owned by the firm

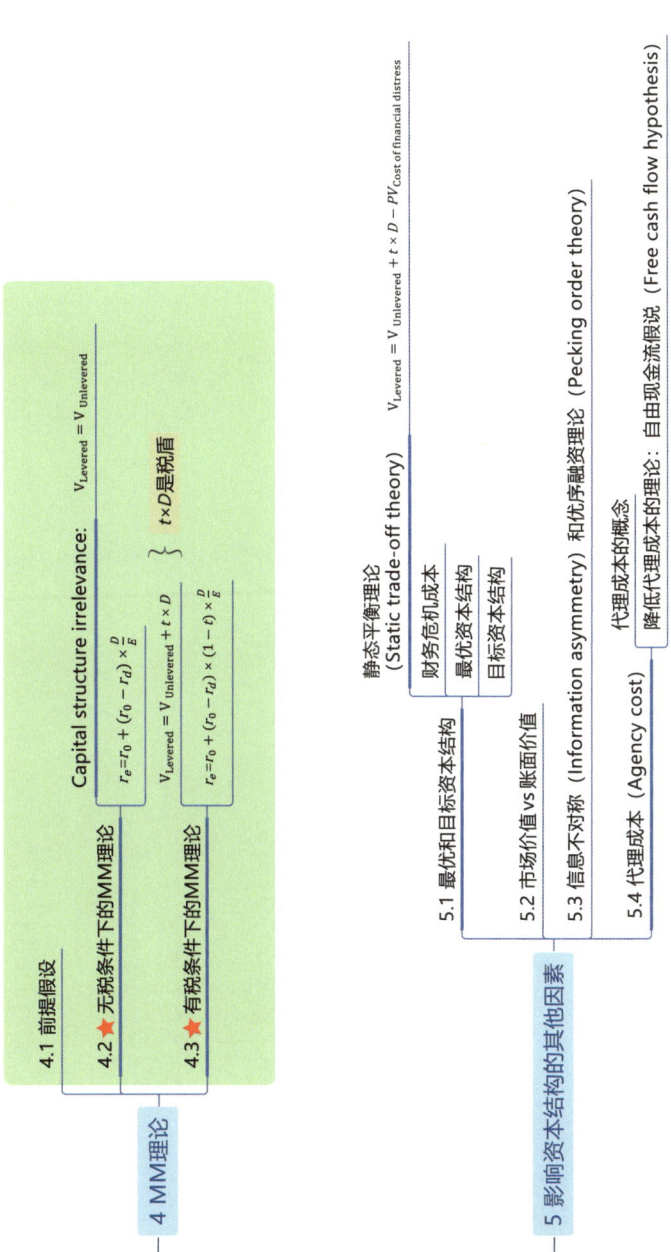

第五部分 权益投资

Reading 34　Market Organization and Structure

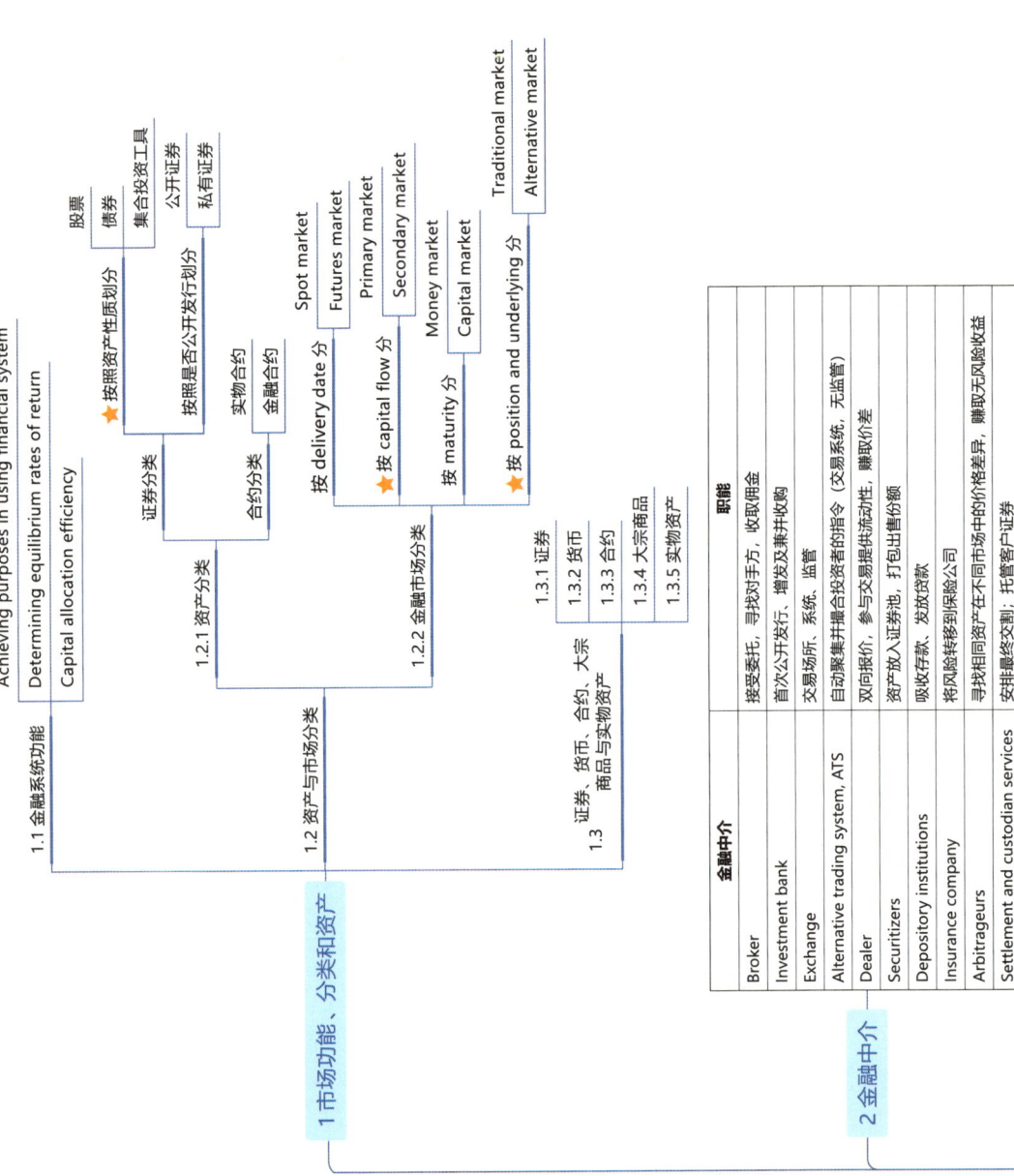

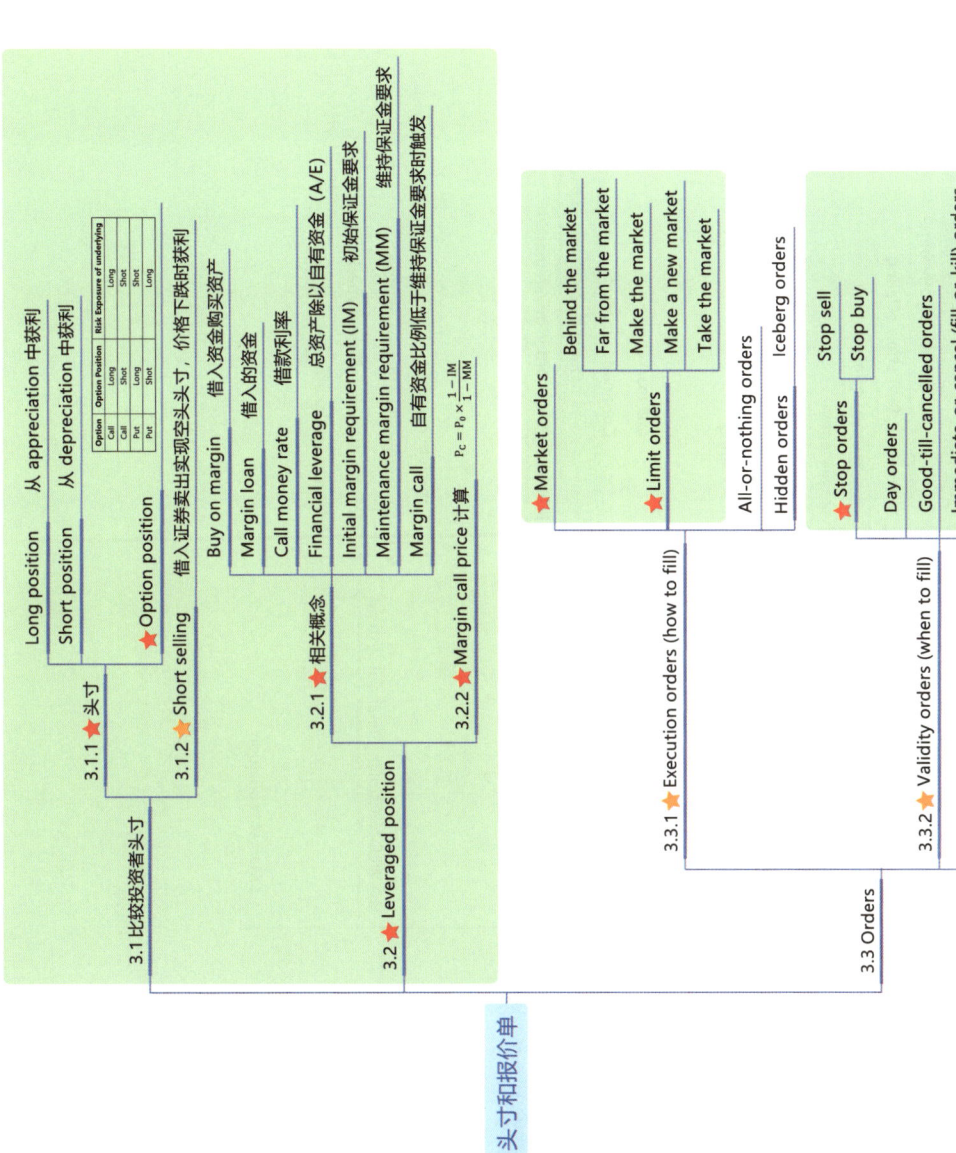

(见上页)

4 一级市场和二级市场

- **4.1 ★ Primary market**
  - 4.1.1 ★ Public offering
    - IPO
      - Underwritten offering
      - Best effort offering
    - Seasoned offering
  - 4.1.2 ★ Others
    - Private placement
    - Shelf registration
    - Dividend reinvestment plan
    - Rights offering
- **4.2 Secondary market**
  - 4.2.1 按 trading session 分
    - Call market
    - Continuous market
  - 4.2.2 按 execution mechanism 分
    - Quote/Price-driven market
    - Order-driven market
    - Brokered market
- **4.3 Well-functioning financial systems**
  - 4.3.1 Complete market
  - 4.3.2 Operationally efficient market
  - 4.3.3 Informationally efficient market
  - 4.3.4 Allocationally efficient market
- **4.4 Market regulation**

Reading 35 Security Market Indexes

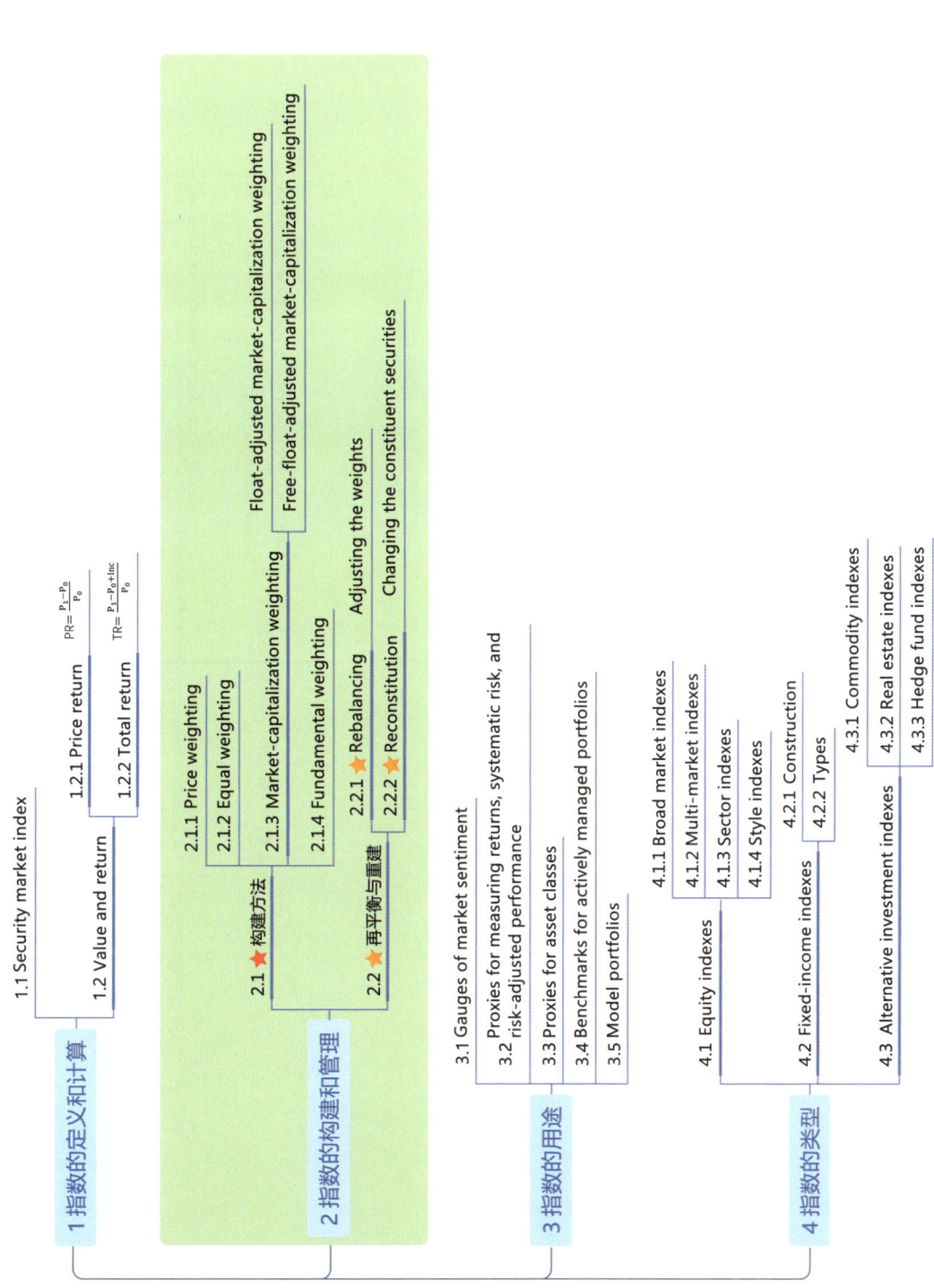

Reading 36　Market Efficiency

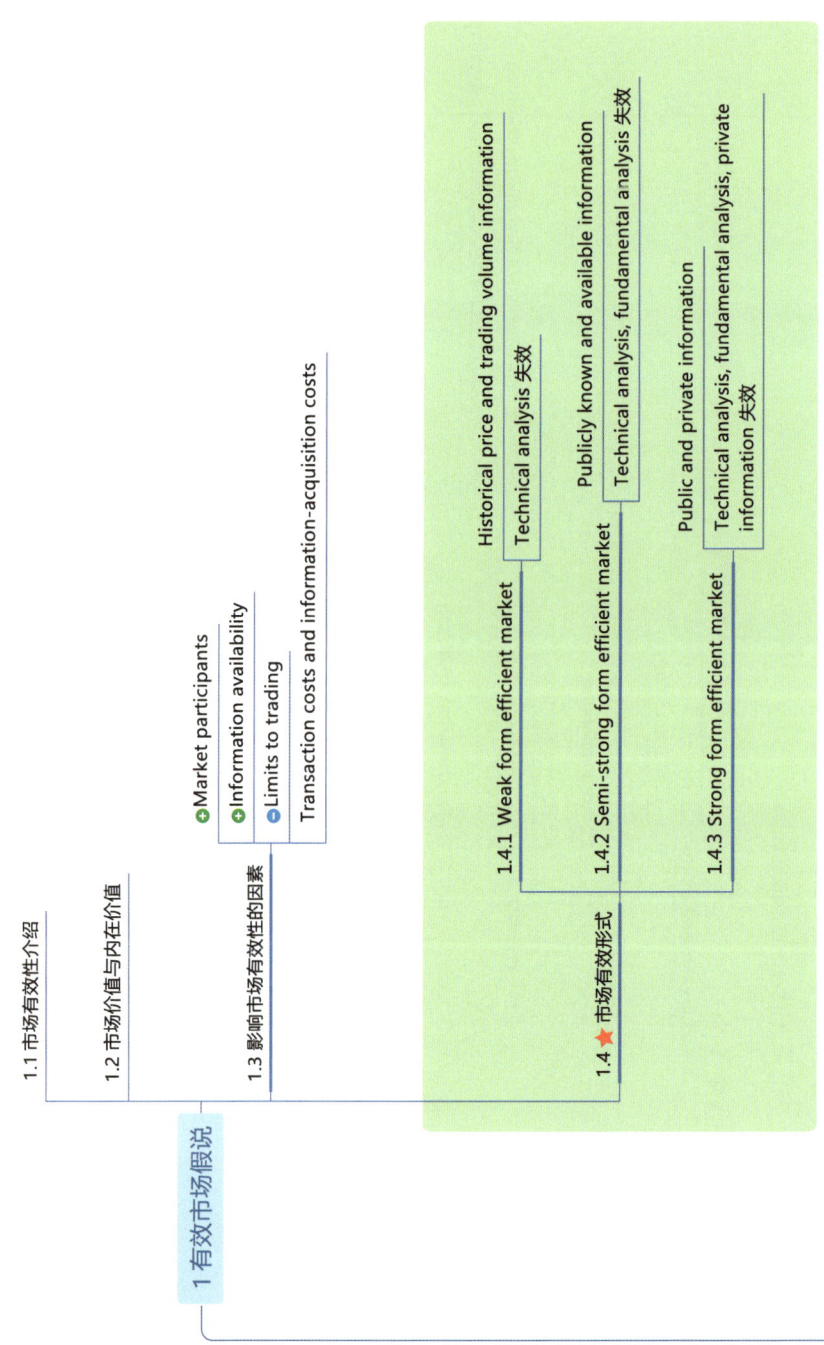

2 市场异常

2.1 ★ 时间序列异常
- 2.1.1 Calendar anomaly
  - January effect
    - Tax-loss selling
    - Window dressing
- 2.1.2 Momentum and overreaction

2.2 ★ 横截面异常
- 2.2.1 Size effect
- 2.2.2 Value effect

2.3 ★ 其他异常
- 2.3.1 Close-ended fund discount
- 2.3.2 Earning surprise
- 2.3.3 IPOs

3 ★ 行为金融

- Loss aversion
- Herding effect
- Overconfidence
- Information cascade
- Representative bias
- Mental accounting
- Conservatism
- Narrow framing

Reading 37　Overview of Equity Securities

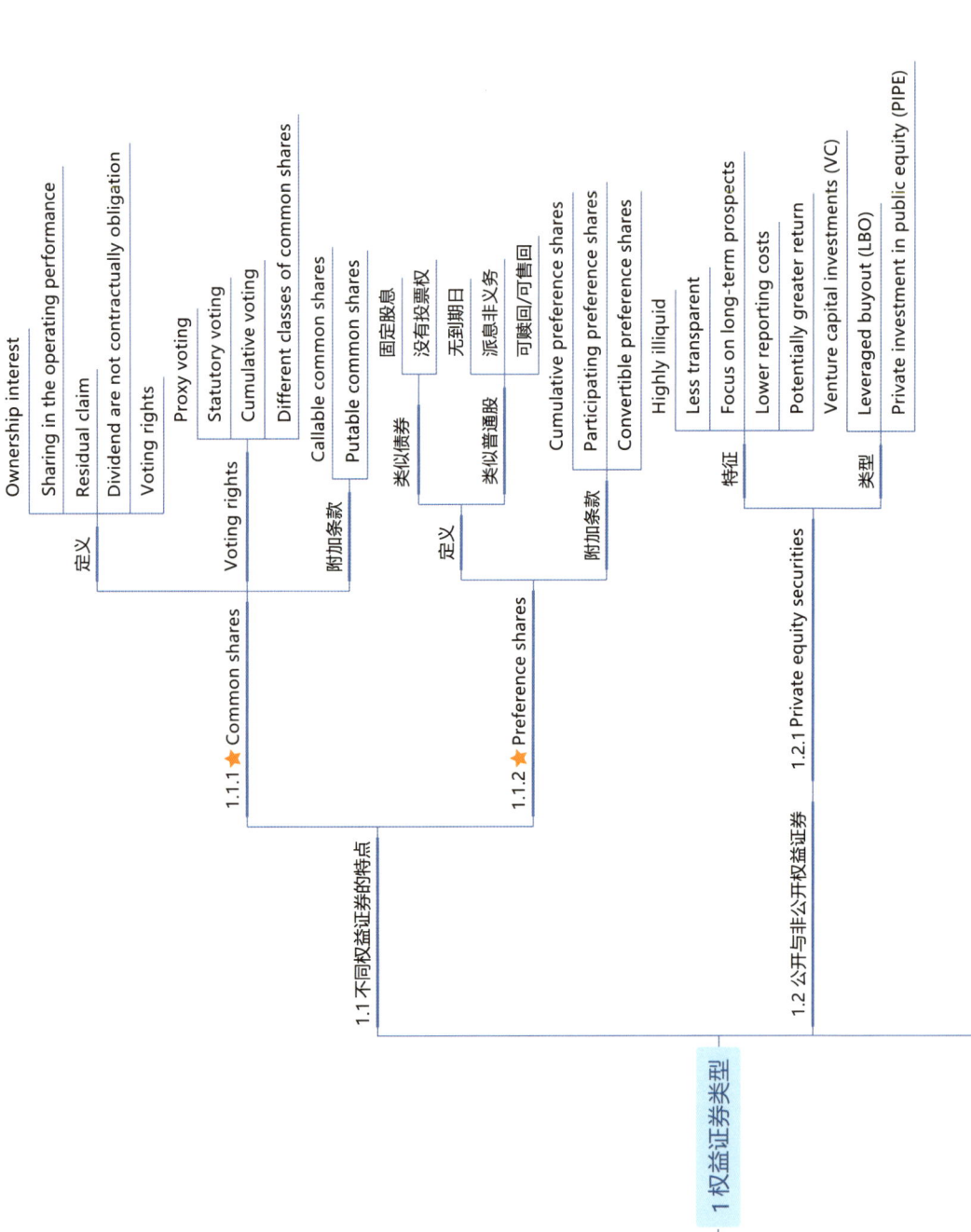

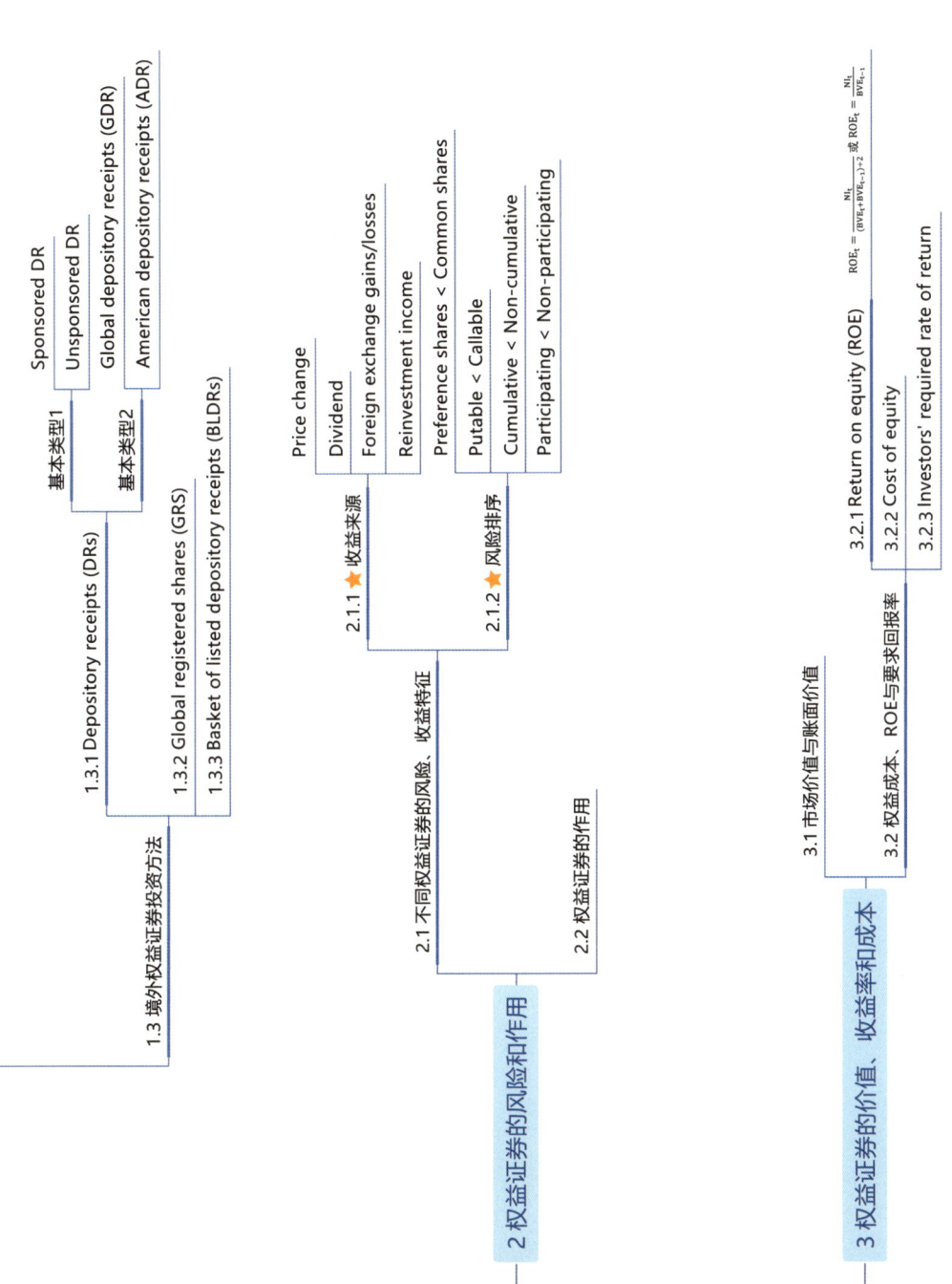

Reading 38　Introduction to Industry and Company Analysis

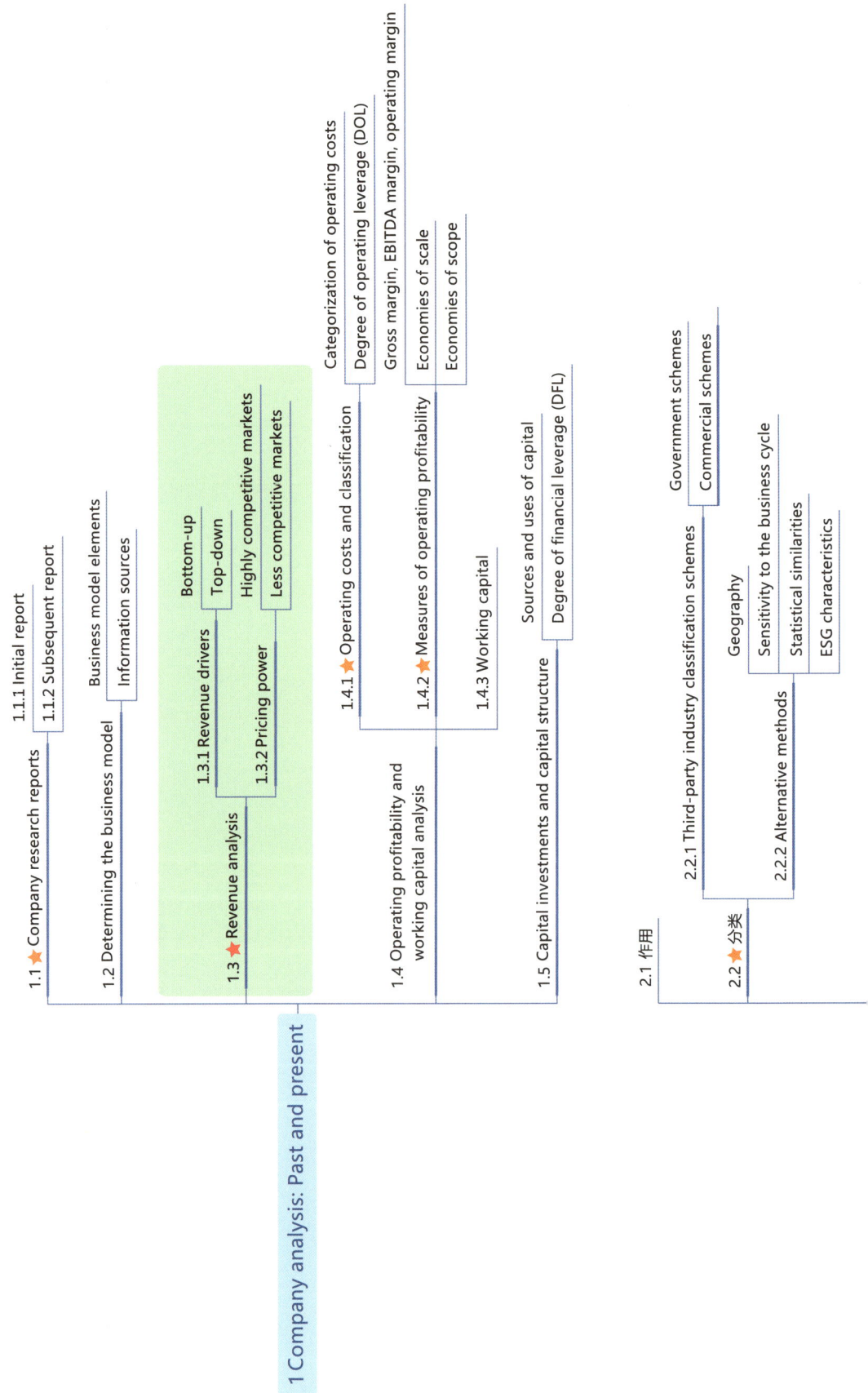

2 Industry and competitive analysis

- 2.3 Industry survey
  - Industry size and historical growth rate
  - Characterizing industry growth
  - Industry profitability measures
  - ★ Market share trends and major players — HHI
- 2.4 ★ Industry structure and external influences
  - 2.4.1 Porter's five forces & Industry structure
  - 2.4.2 PESTLE analysis & External influences
- 2.5 ★ Competitive strategy
  - Cost leadership
  - Differentiation
  - Focus

3 Company analysis: Forecasting

- 3.1 预测对象、原则和方法
  - 预测对象
  - 预测方法
  - Selecting a forecast horizon
- 3.2 Forecasting revenues
  - 3.2.1 ★ 收入的预测对象
    - Historical results: Assume past is precedent
    - Historical base rates and convergence
    - Management guidance
    - Analyst's discretionary forecast
  - 3.2.2 收入的预测方法
    - Top-down drivers
    - Bottom-up drivers
- 3.3 Forecasting operating expenses and working capital
- 3.4 Forecasting capital investments and capital structure
  - Forecasting capital investments
    - Maintenance capital expenditures
    - Growth capital expenditures
  - Forecasting capital structure
- 3.5 Scenario analysis

Reading 39　Equity Valuation: Concepts and Basic Tools

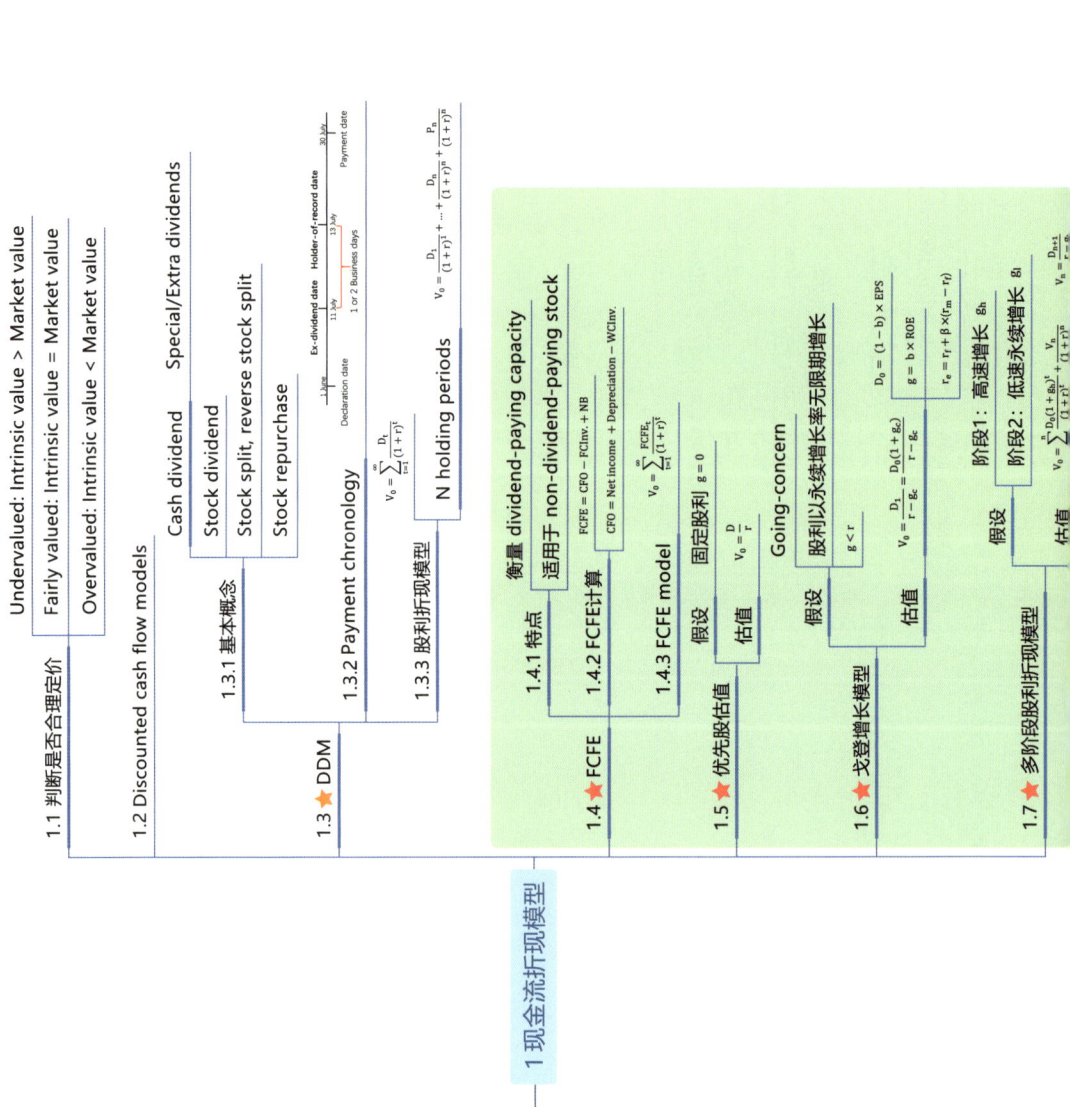

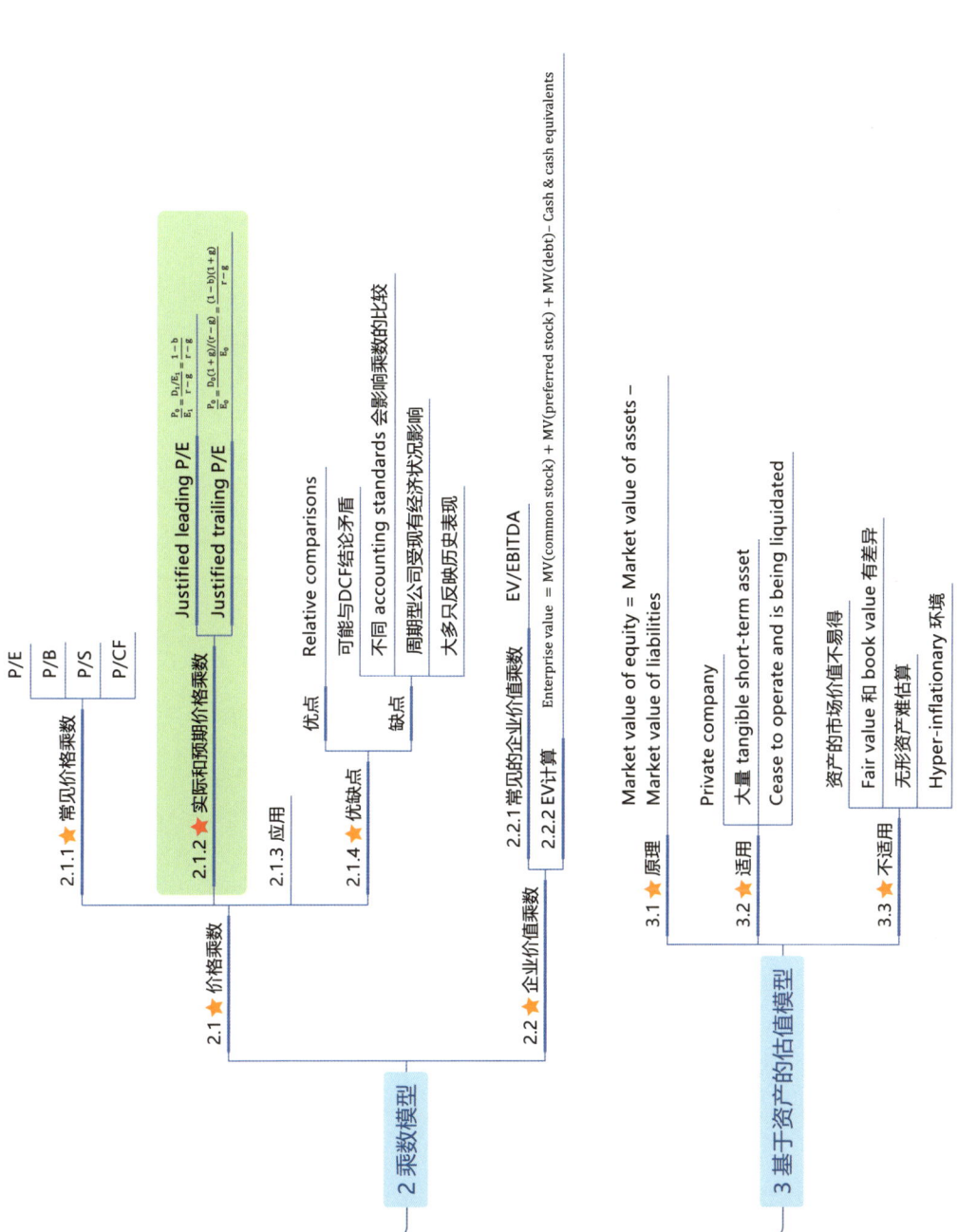

第六部分 固定收益证券

Reading 40　Fixed-Income Securities

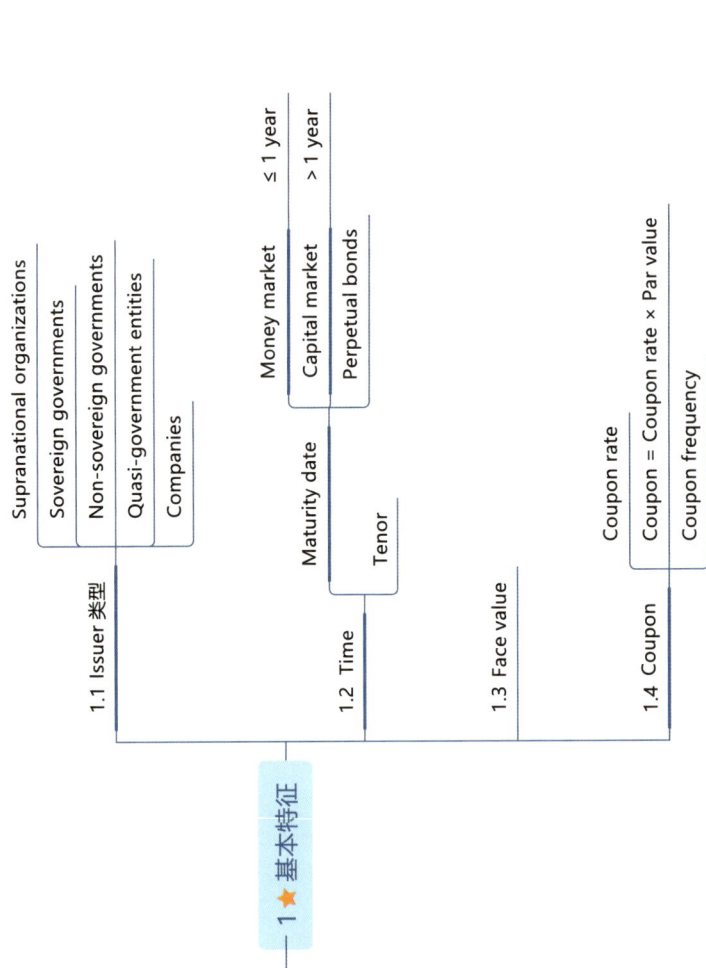

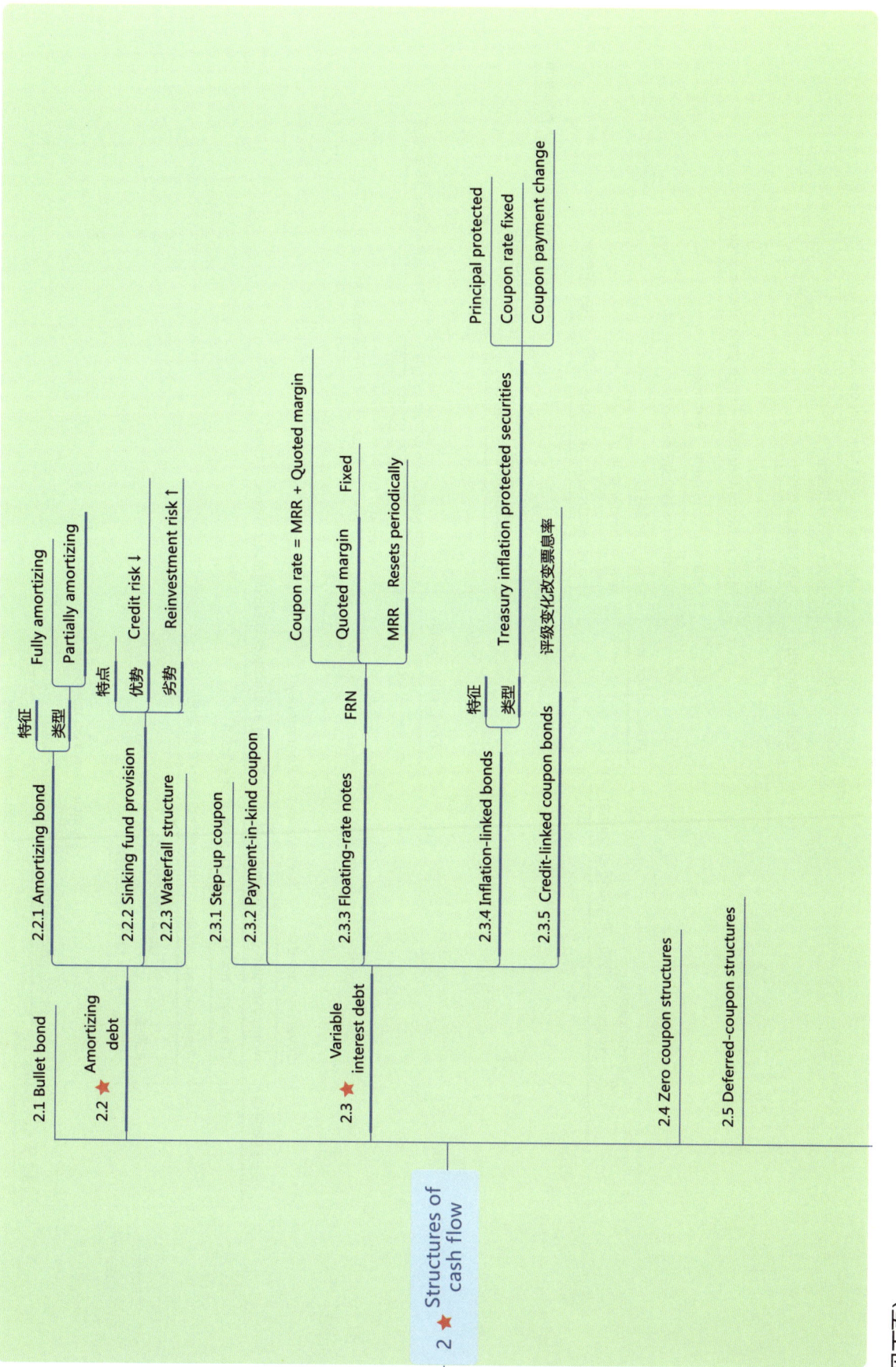

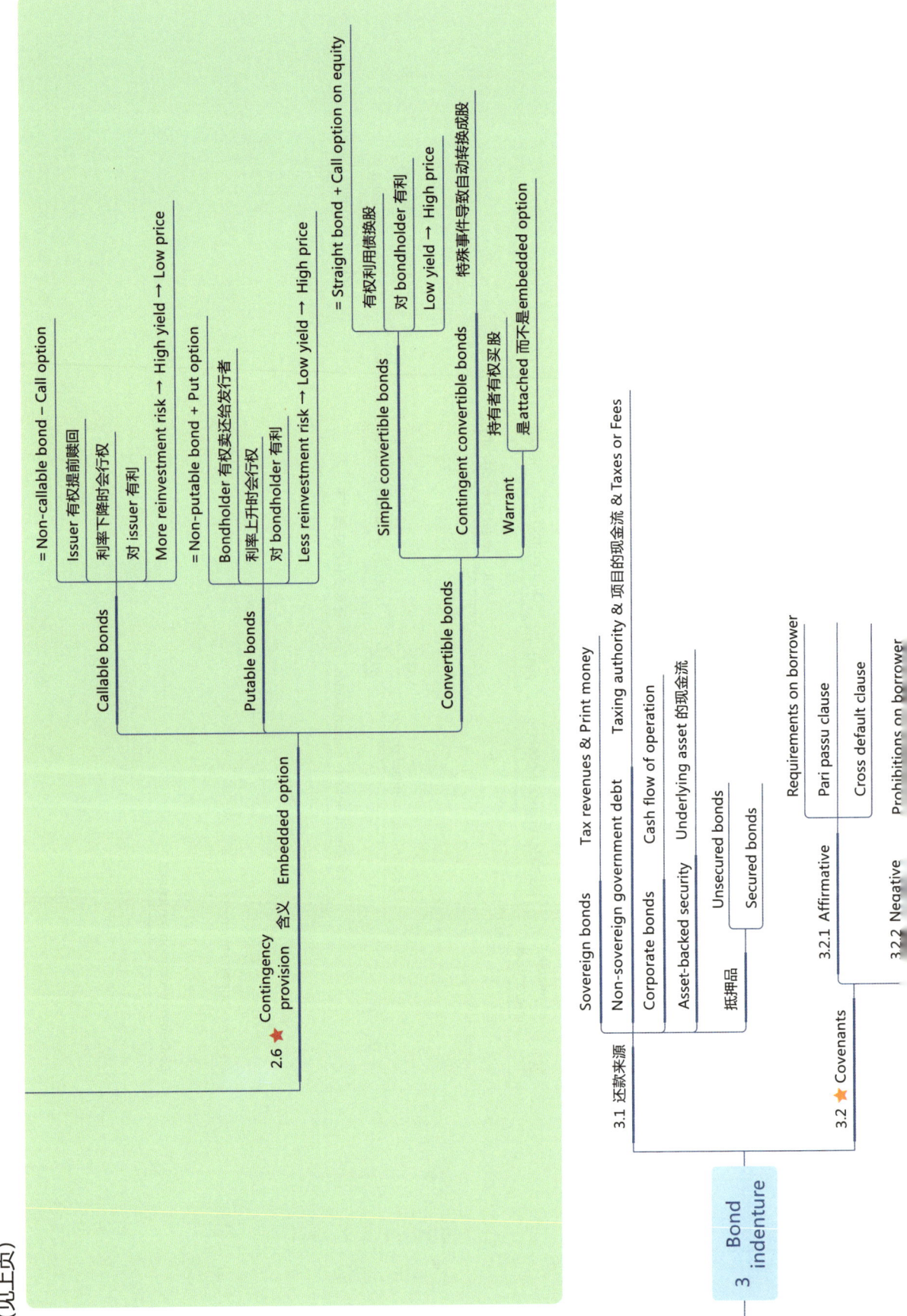

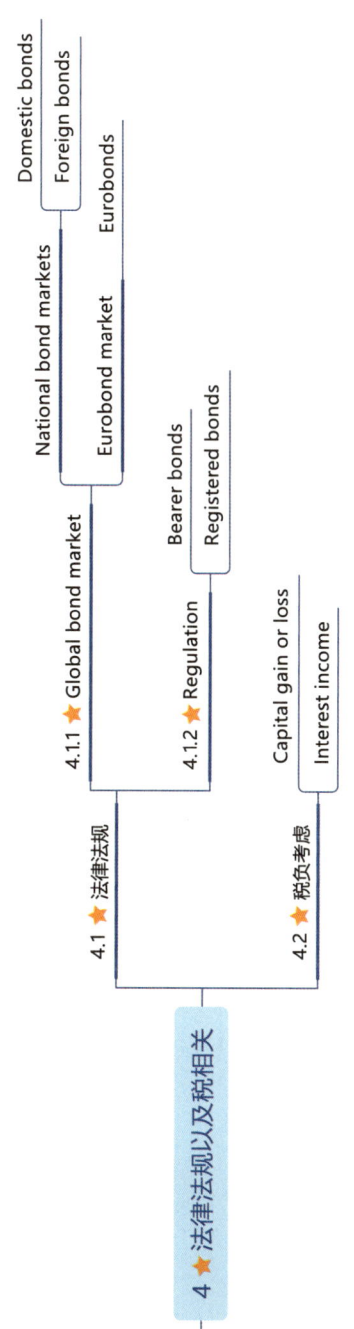

Reading 41 Fixed-Income Markets

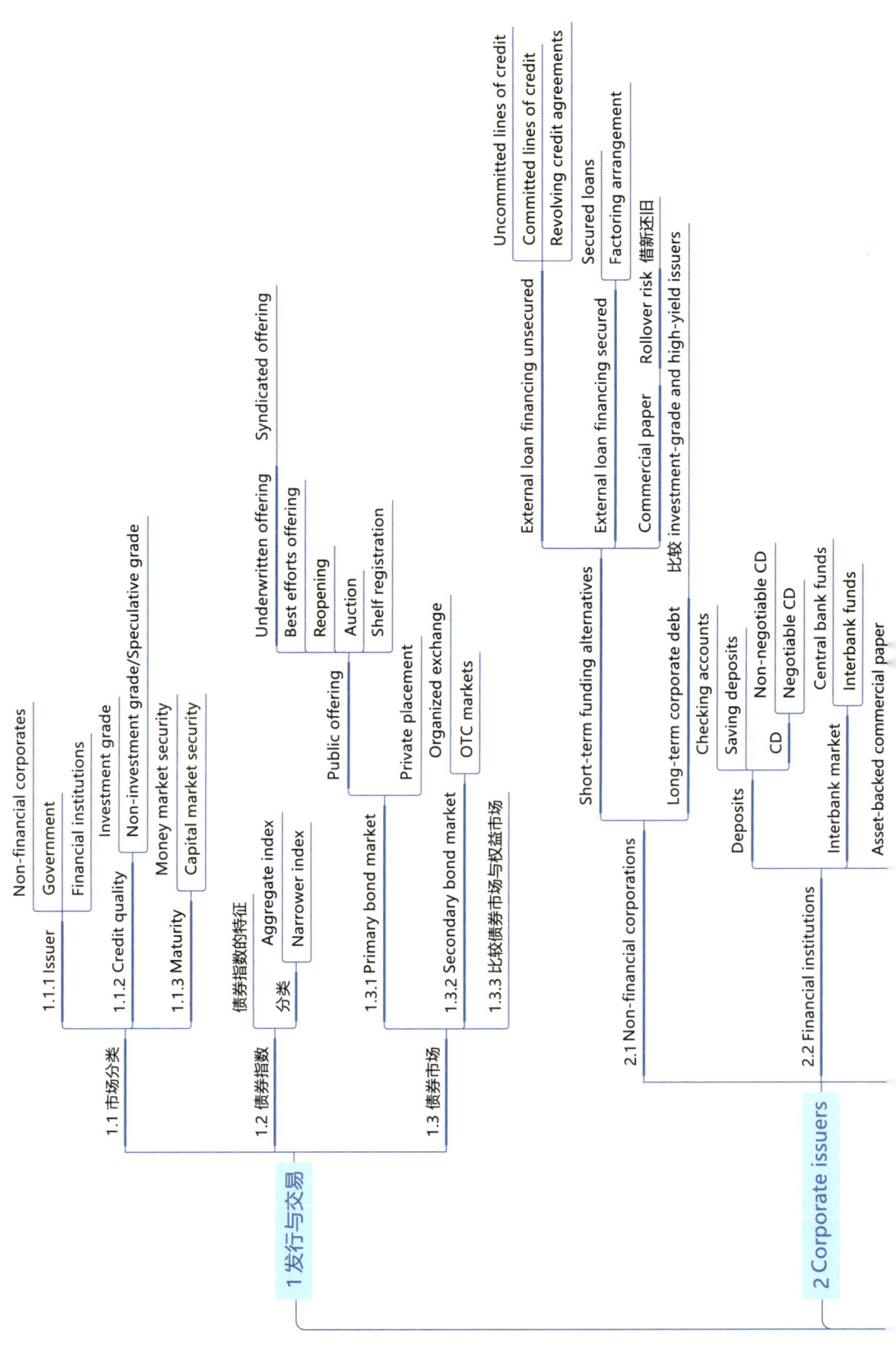

2.3 ★ 回购协议 (Repurchase agreement, Repo)

- **定义**
  - General collateral repo
  - Reverse repurchase agreements
- **回购协议流程图**
- **Initial margin 计算**
  $$\text{Initial margin} = \frac{\text{Security Price}_0}{\text{Purchase Price}_0}$$
- **Repo rate**
  - 计算
    $$\text{Repurchase price} = \text{Purchase price}_0 \times \left(1 + \frac{\text{repo term}}{360} \times \text{repo rate}\right)$$
  - 影响因素 $\Big\}$ Repo rate 高
    - 回购期长
    - 抵押品未交割
    - 抵押品信用质量差
    - 抵押品供过于求
    - 其他融资来源成本高
- **Repo margin/Haircut**
  - 计算
    $$\text{Haircut} = \frac{\text{Security Price}_0 - \text{Purchase Price}_0}{\text{Security Price}_0}$$
  - 影响因素 $\Big\}$ Repo margin 高
    - 回购期长
    - 抵押品信用质量差
    - 借款者信用质量差
    - 抵押品供过于求
- **应用与风险管理**
  - 应用目的
  - 五种风险
    - Default risk
    - Collateral risk
    - Margining risk
    - Legal risk
    - Netting and settlement risk

3 Government issuers

3.1 ★ Sovereign debt

- ★ Sovereign bonds 的定义
  - On-the-run
  - U.S. Treasuries
    - T-Bills
    - T-Notes
    - T-Bonds
- ★ Emerging market sovereign bonds
  - Direct currency risk
  - Indirect currency risk
- ★ Government's choice on bond maturity
  - 政府主权债务的发行
    - Auction
      - Single-price auction
      - Multiple-price auction
    - Non-economic objectives
  - 政府主权债务的交易

3.2 Other government-related debts

- Local government bonds
- Quasi-government bonds/ Agency bonds
- Supranational bonds

Reading 42 Fixed-Income Valuation

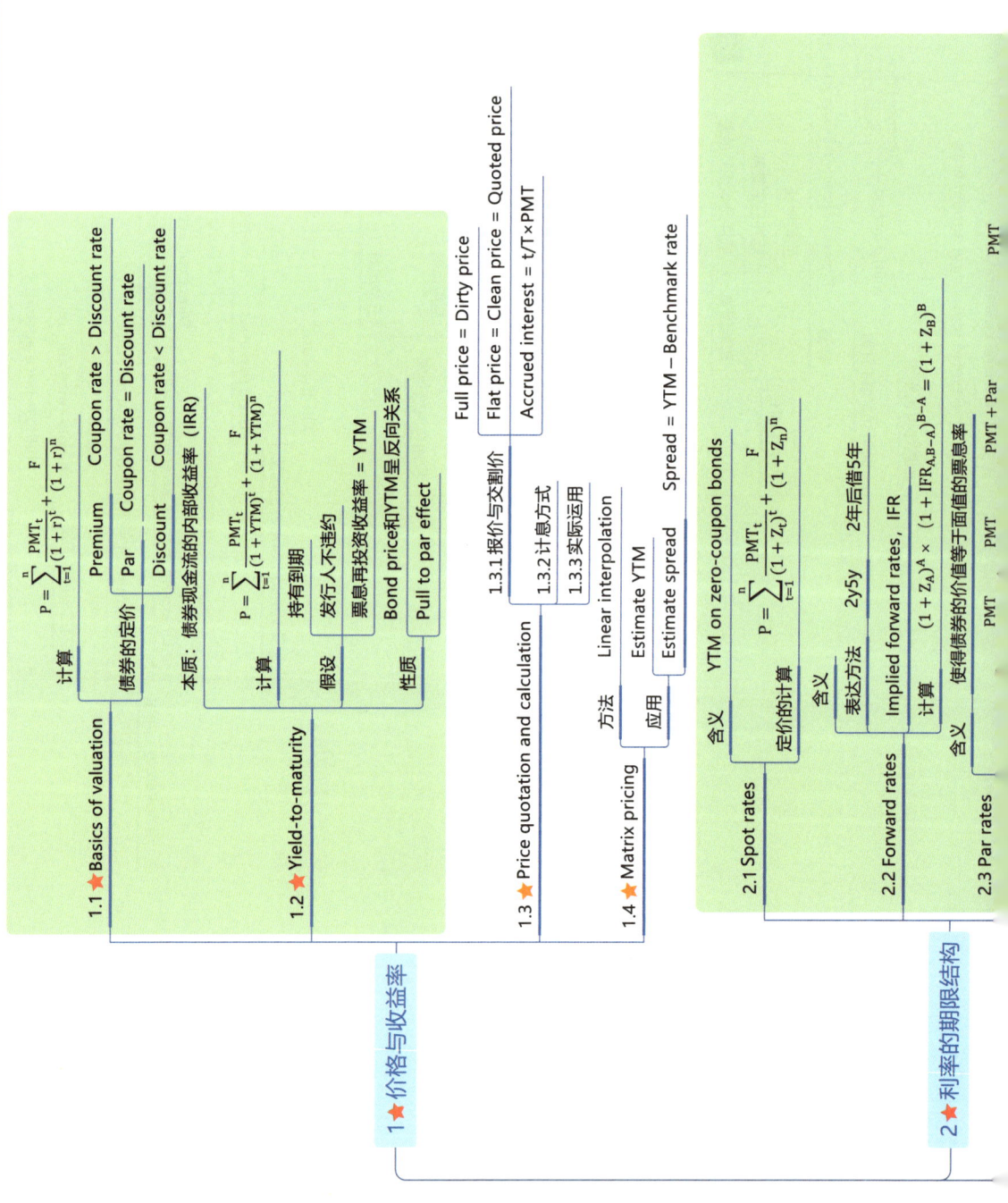

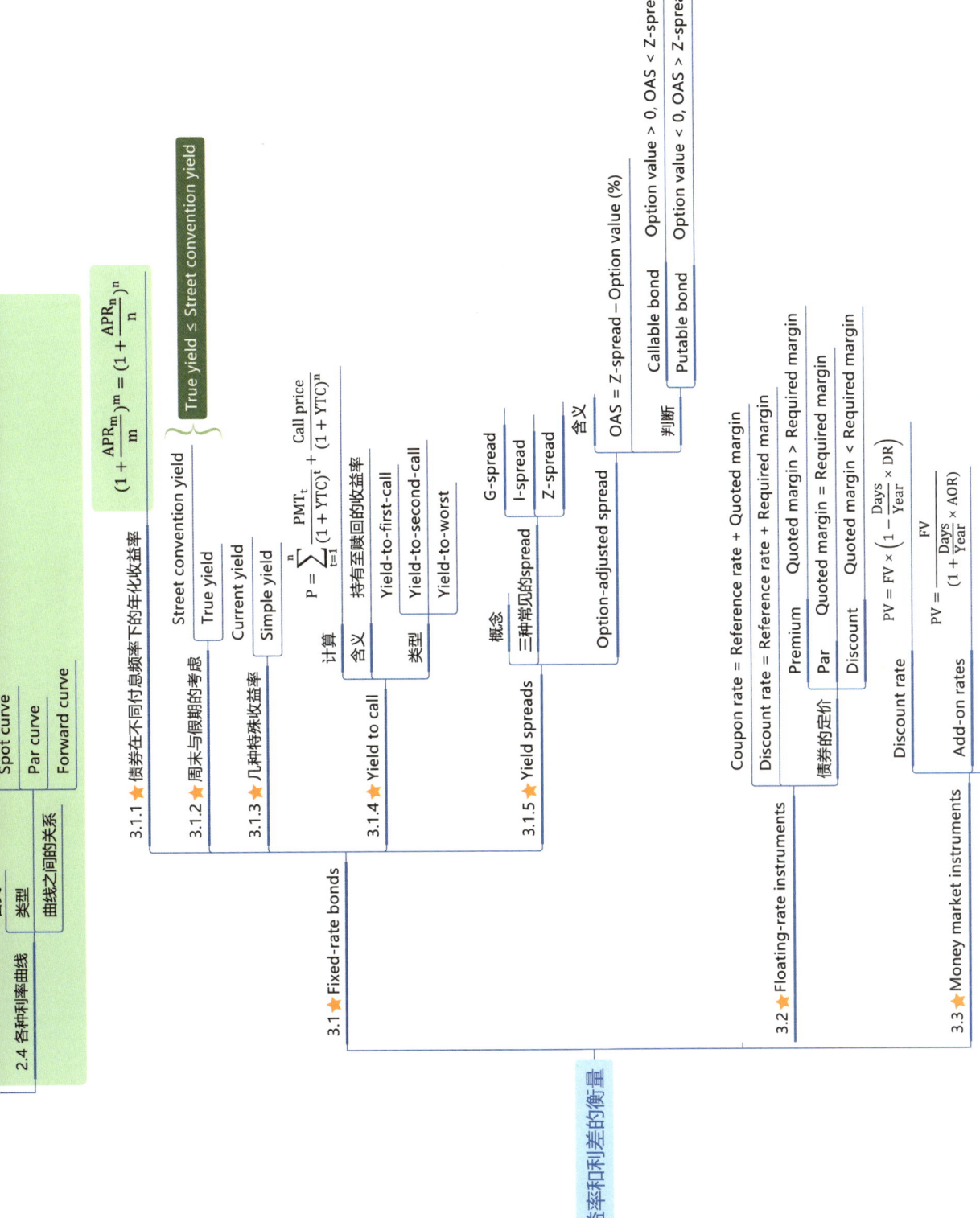

Reading 43 Interest Rate Risk

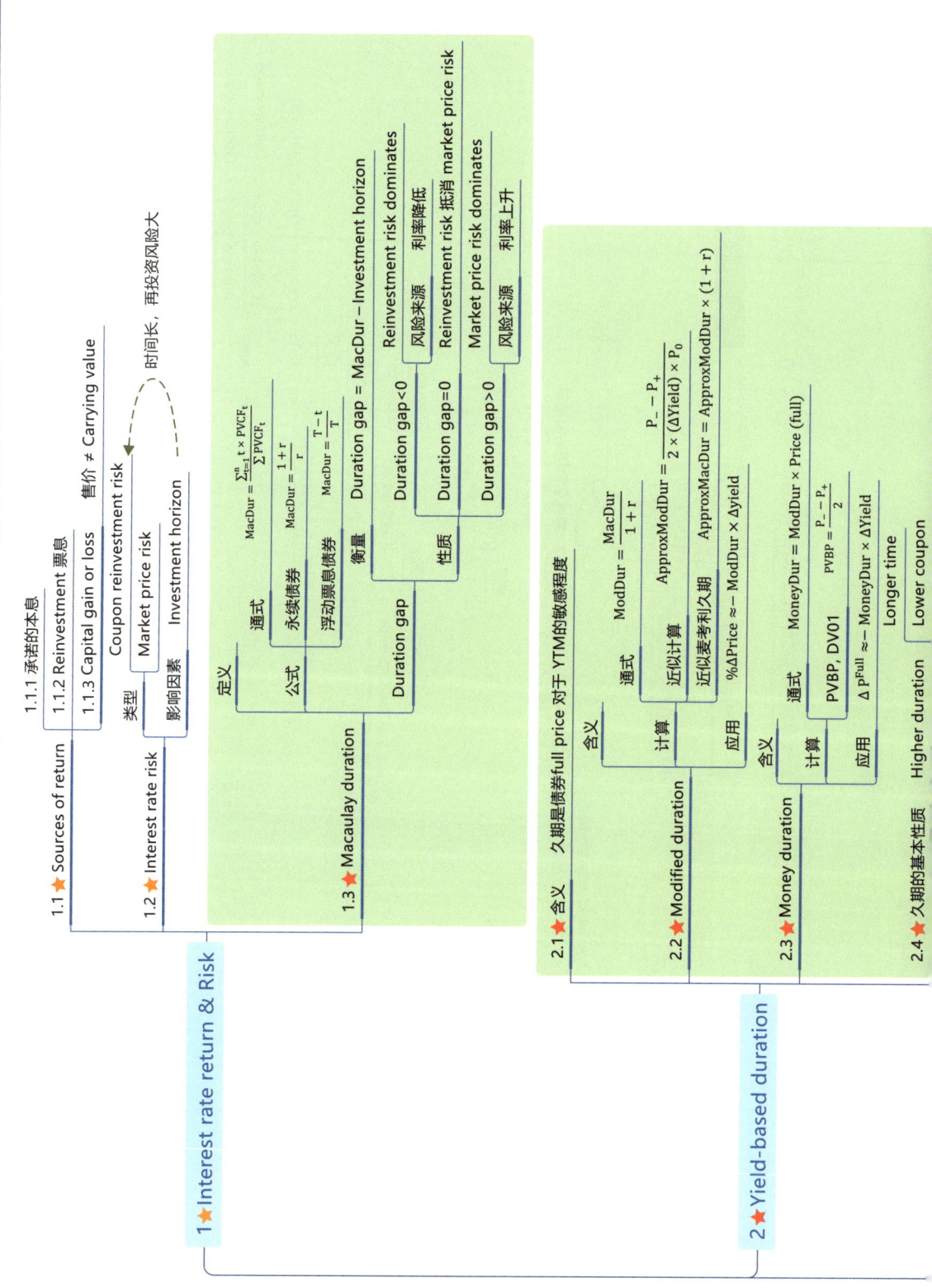

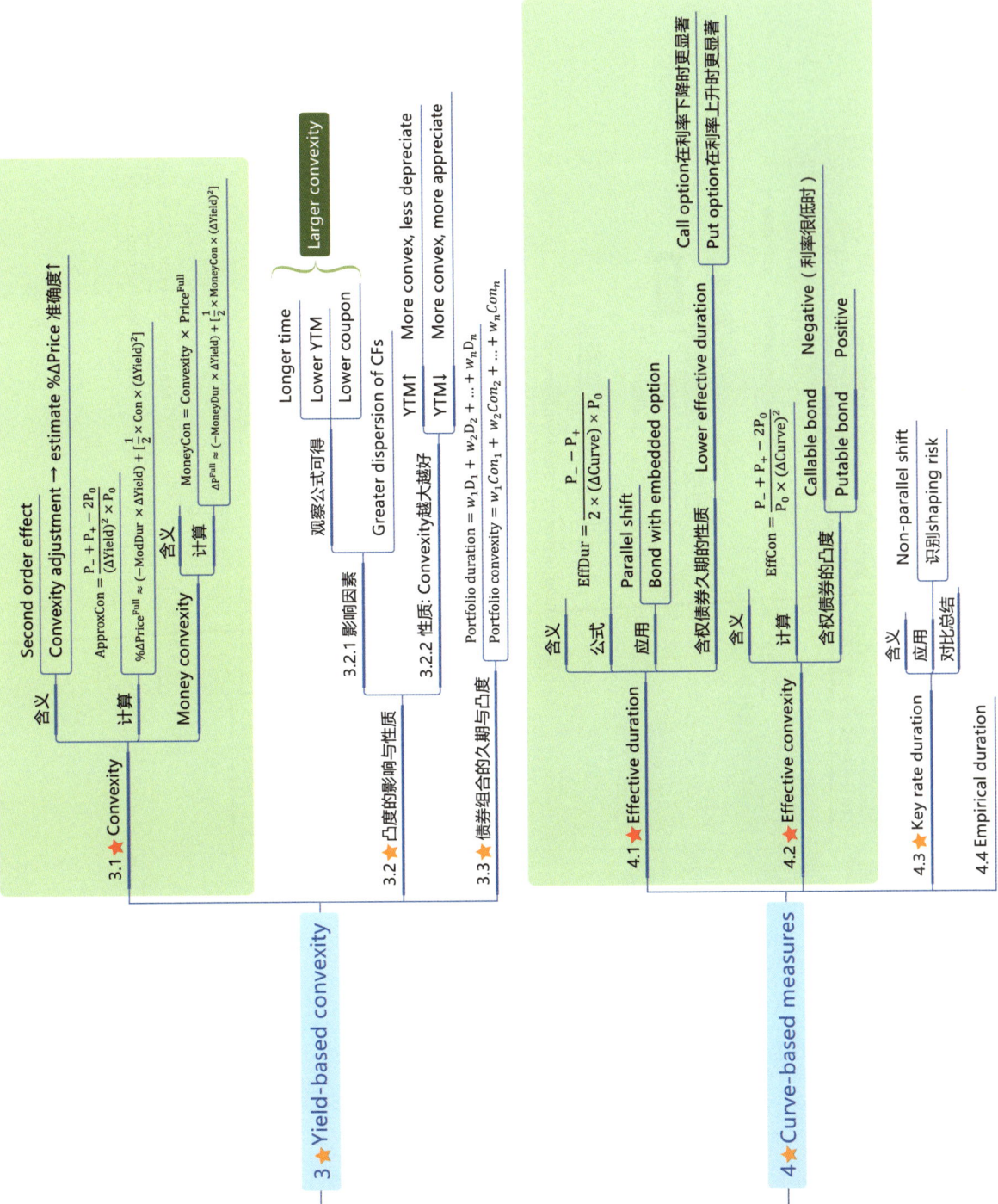

Reading 44 Credit Risk

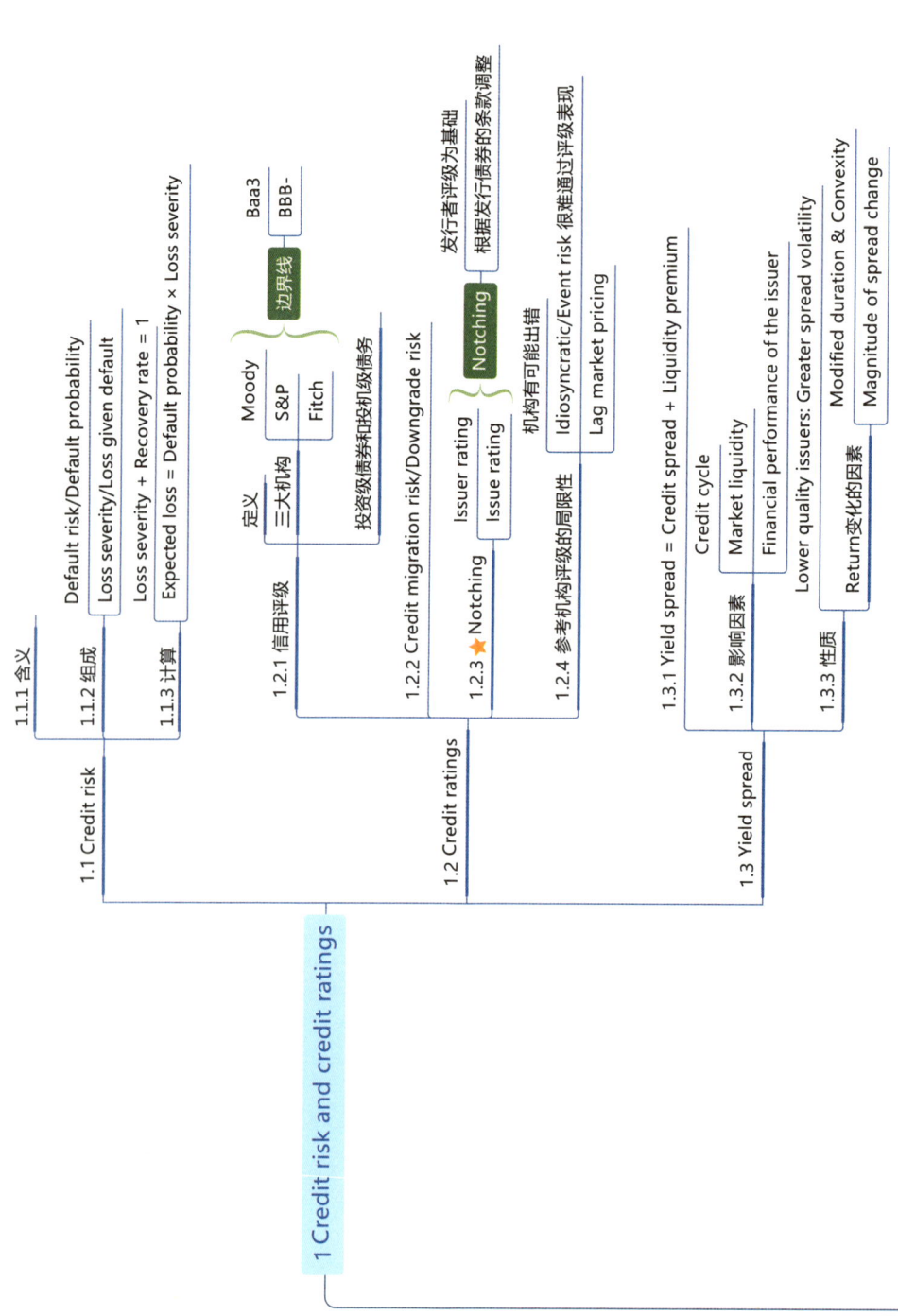

第六部分 固定收益证券 | 81

Credit analysis 2 for government issuers

- 2.1 [Sovereign bond]
  - 重要因素
    - 总感更重要，政府很通过本币发行可以解决
    - Willingness
  - 2.2 Sovereign credit analysis
    - 定性因素
      - Government institutions and policy
      - Fiscal flexibility
      - Monetary effectiveness
      - Economic flexibility
    - 定量因素
      - External status
      - Fiscal strength
      - Economic growth and stability
      - External stability
- 2.3 Municipal debt
  - General obligation bonds
  - Revenue bonds
- 2.4 Municipal debt credit analysis
  - Project analysis
  - Financial analysis

Credit analysis 3 for corporate issuers

- 3.1 Corporate credit analysis
  - 定性因素
    - Business model
    - Industry and competition
    - Corporate governance
  - 定量因素
    - Business risk
    - Financial ratio analysis
- 3.2 ★ Seniority ranking
  - First lien loan
  - Senior secured debt
  - Senior unsecured debt
  - Senior subordinated debt
  - Subordinated debt
  - Junior subordinated debt

Reading 45 Asset-Backed Security

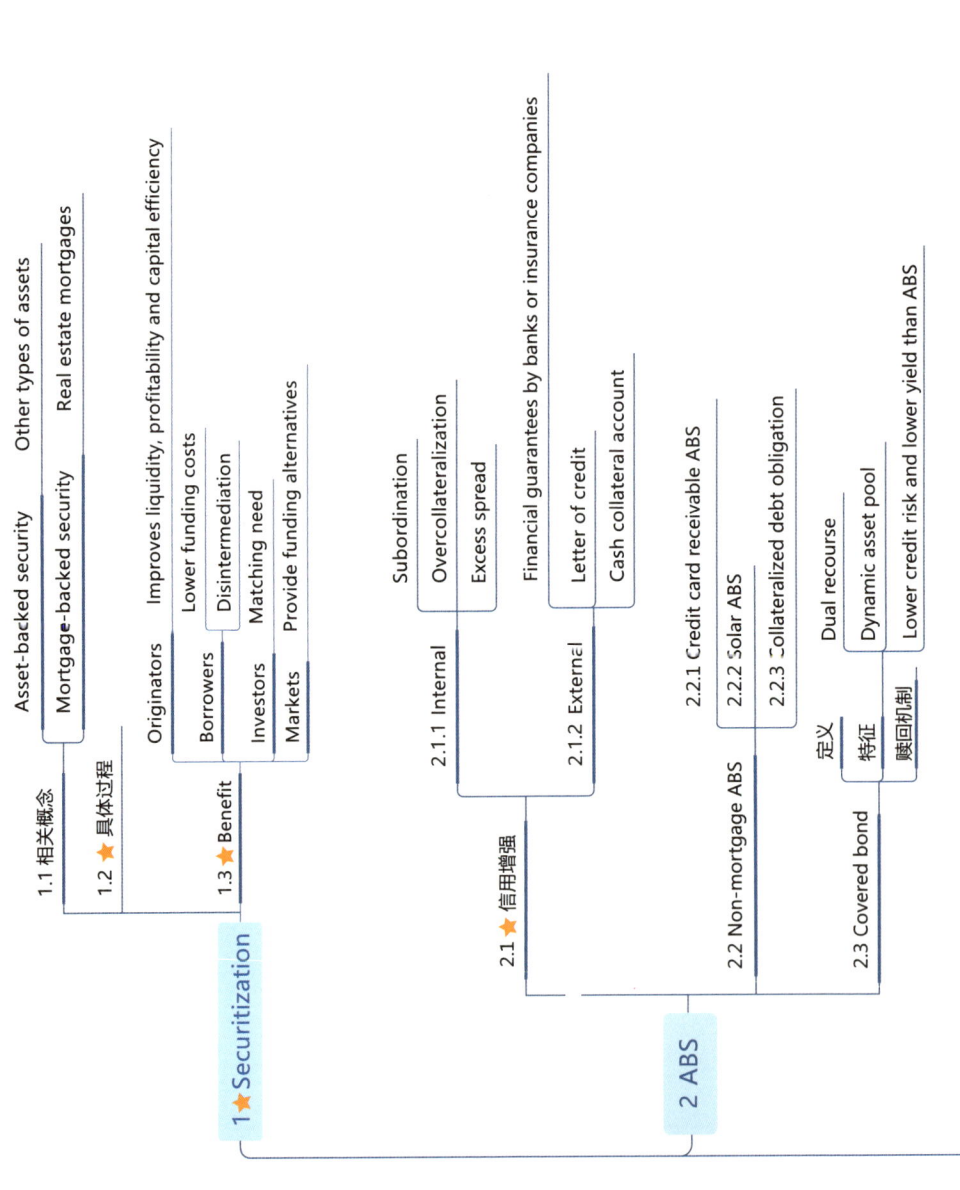

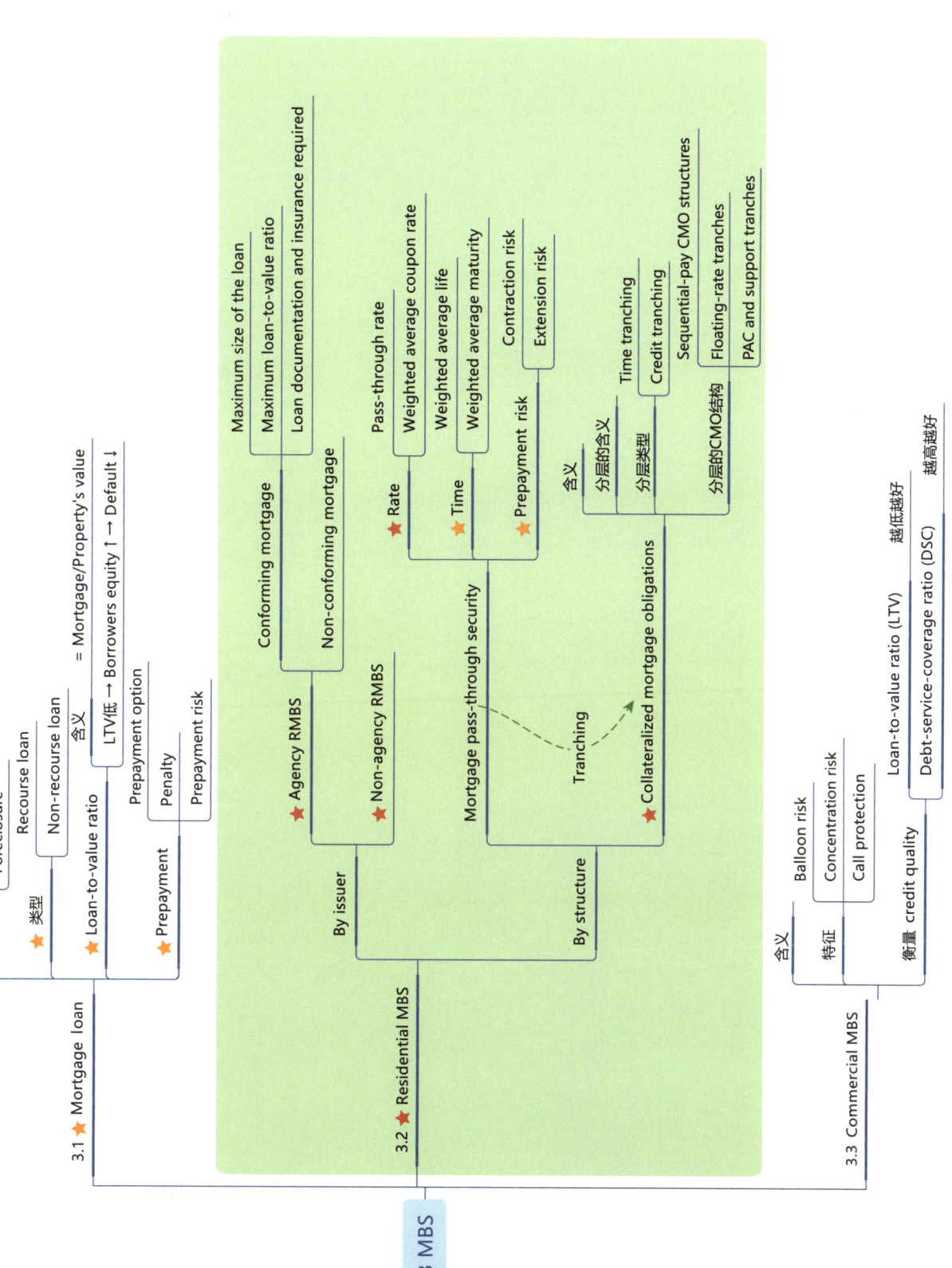

第七部分 衍生品

Reading 46 Derivative Markets and Instruments

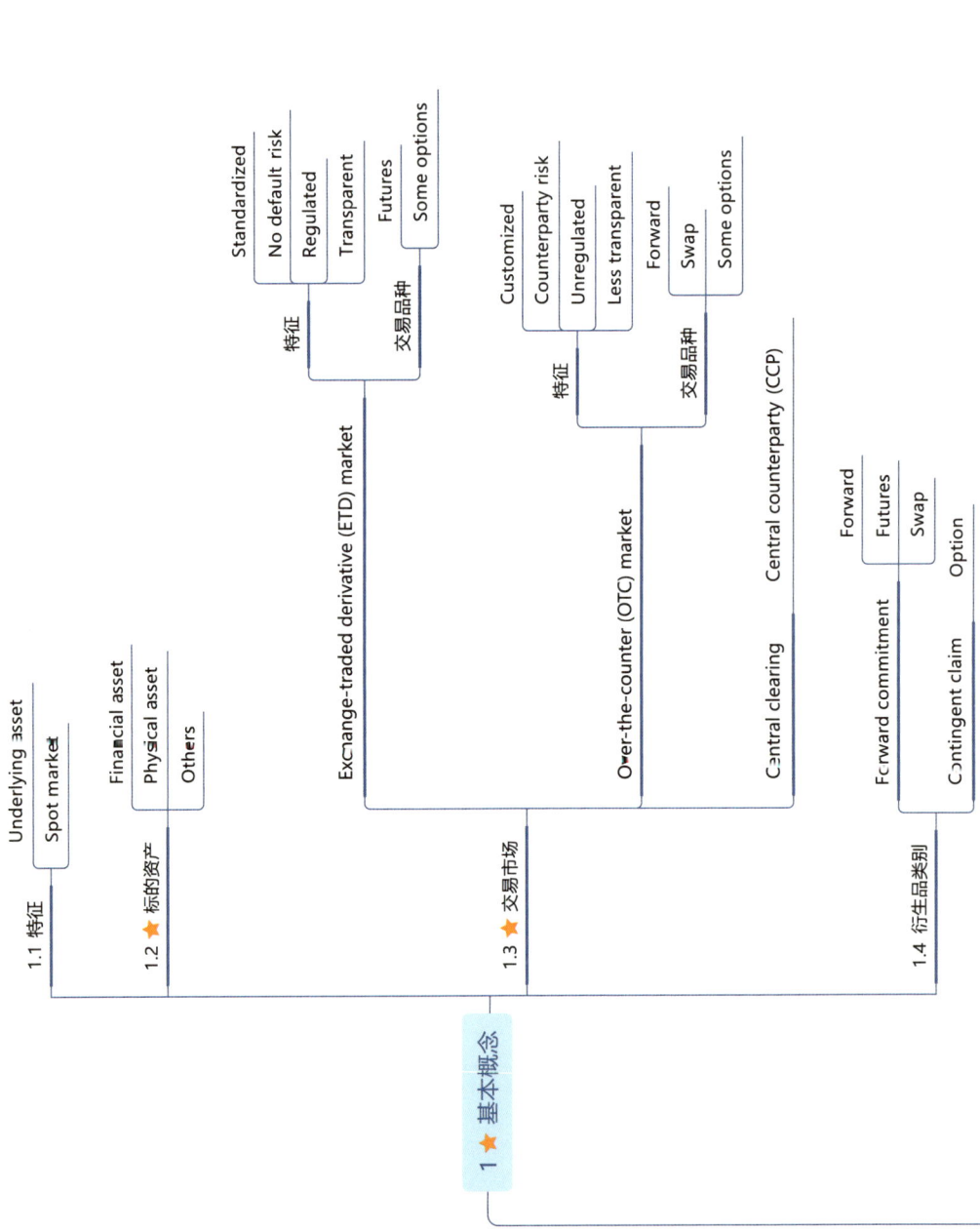

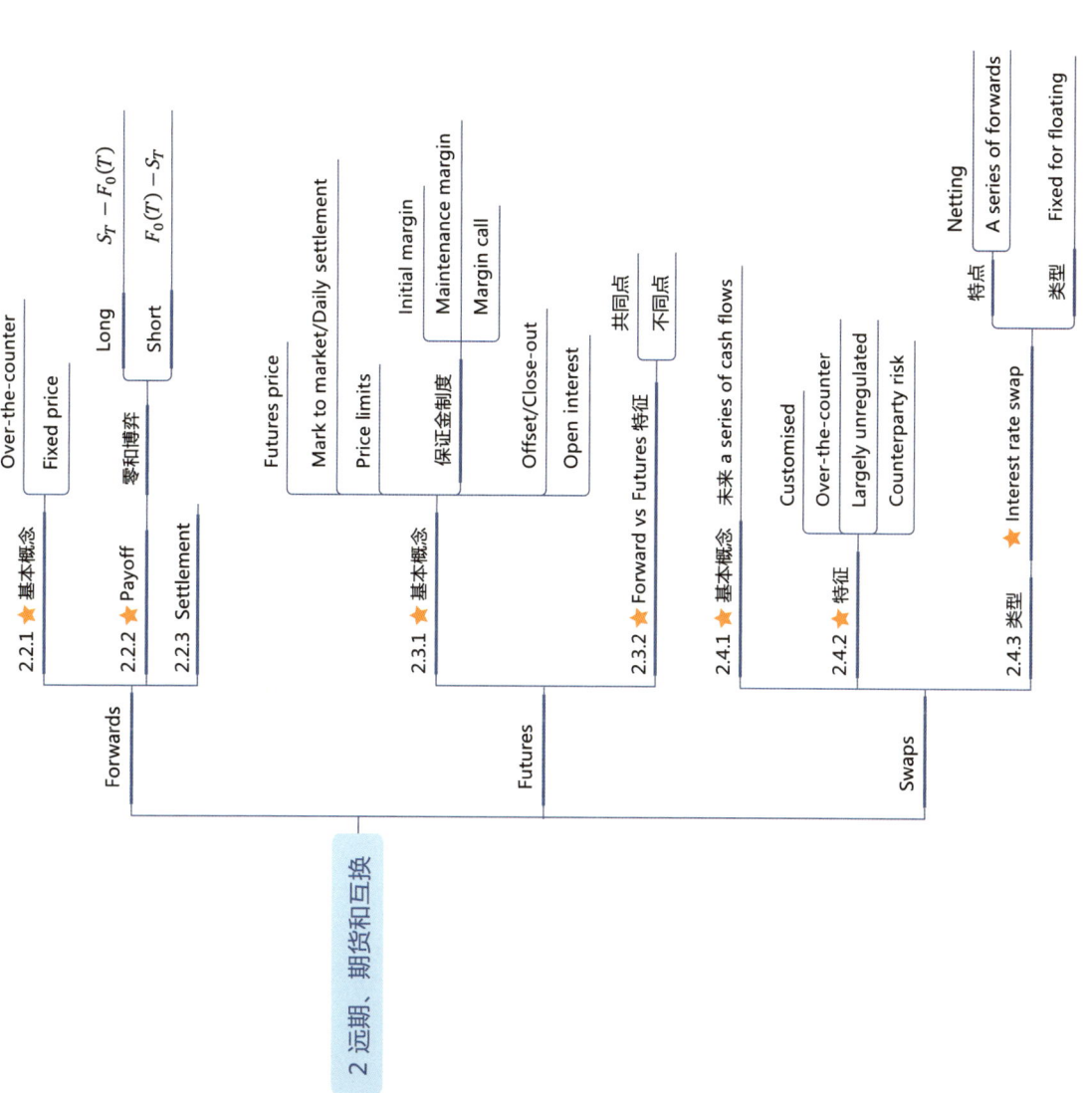

(见上页)

3 期权和信用衍生品

Option

3.1 ★ 基本概念 — 期权的定义
- Option premium = Option price (C_0, P_0)
- Exercise price/Strike price (X)

3.2 ★ 特征
- Right
- Not an obligation

3.3 ★ 类型
- 权利
  - Call option — Buy
  - Put option — Sell
- 可否提前行权
  - ✓ American option
  - ✗ European option

3.4 ★ 收益与利润

Option	Position	Payoff	Profit
Call	Long	$c_T = \max(0, S_T - X)$	$\pi = \max(0, S_T - X) - c_0$
	Short	$-c_T = -\max(0, S_T - X)$	$\pi = -\max(0, S_T - X) + c_0$
Put	Long	$p_T = \max(0, X - S_T)$	$\pi = \max(0, X - S_T) - p_0$
	Short	$-p_T = -\max(0, X - S_T)$	$\pi = -\max(0, X - S_T) + p_0$

3.5 ★ Moneyness

Moneyness	Call option	Put option
In the money	$S > X$	$S < X$
At the money	$S = X$	$S = X$
Out of the money	$S < X$	$S > X$

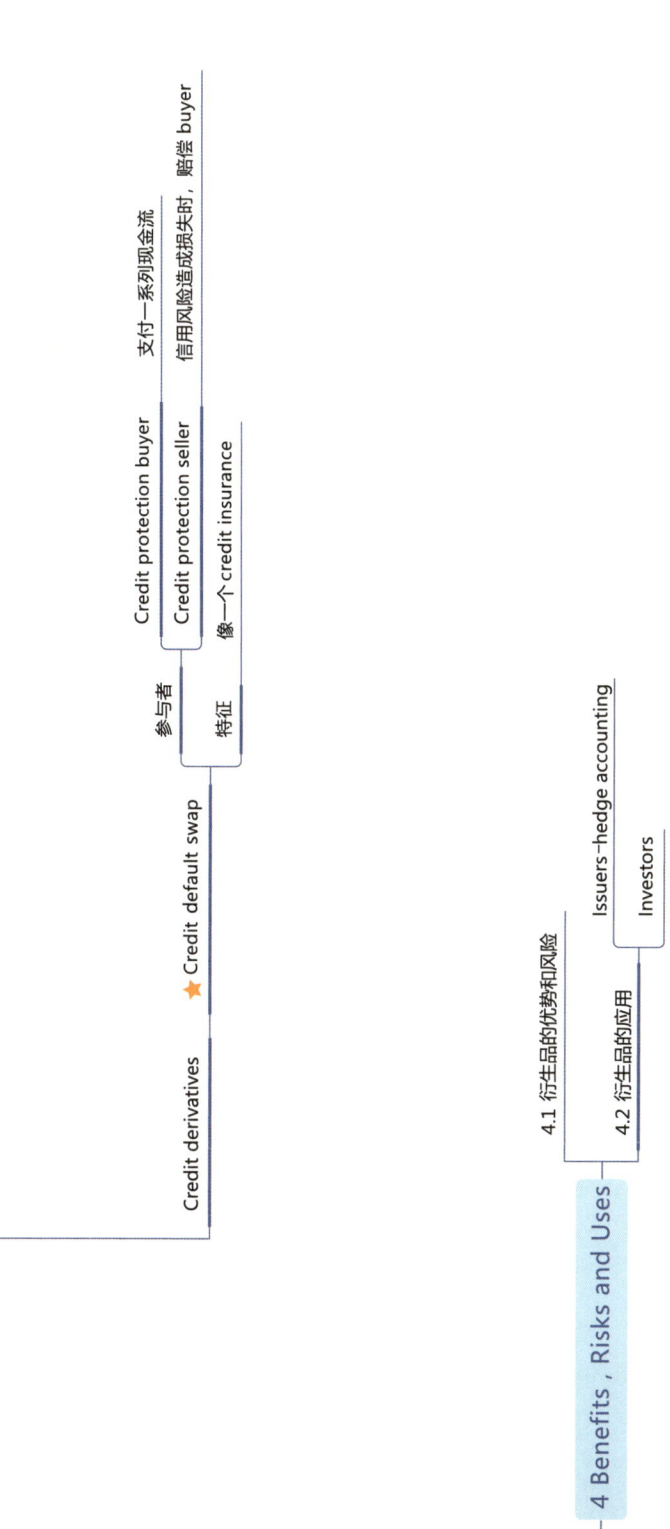

Reading 47 Basics of Derivative Pricing and Valuation

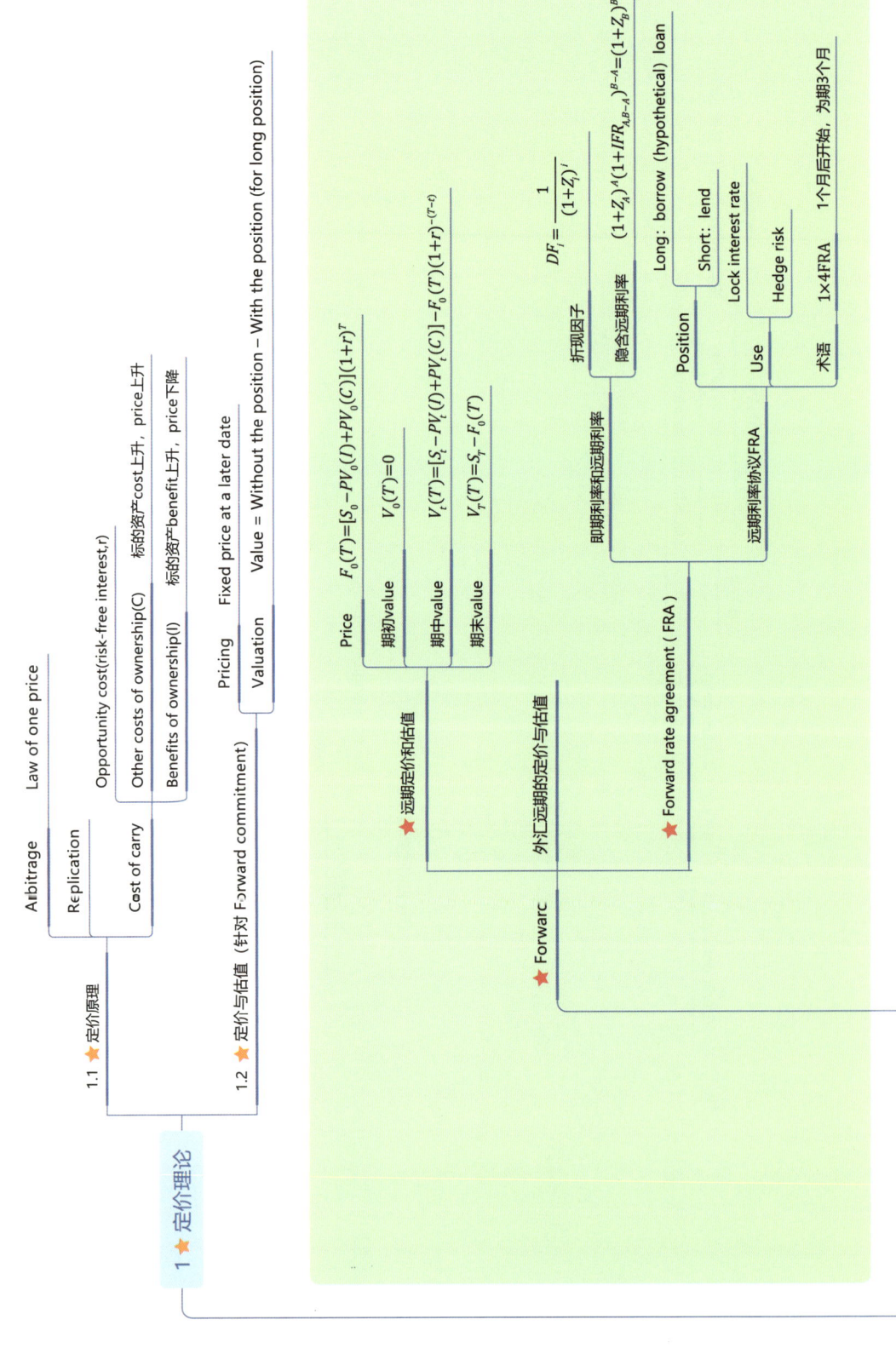

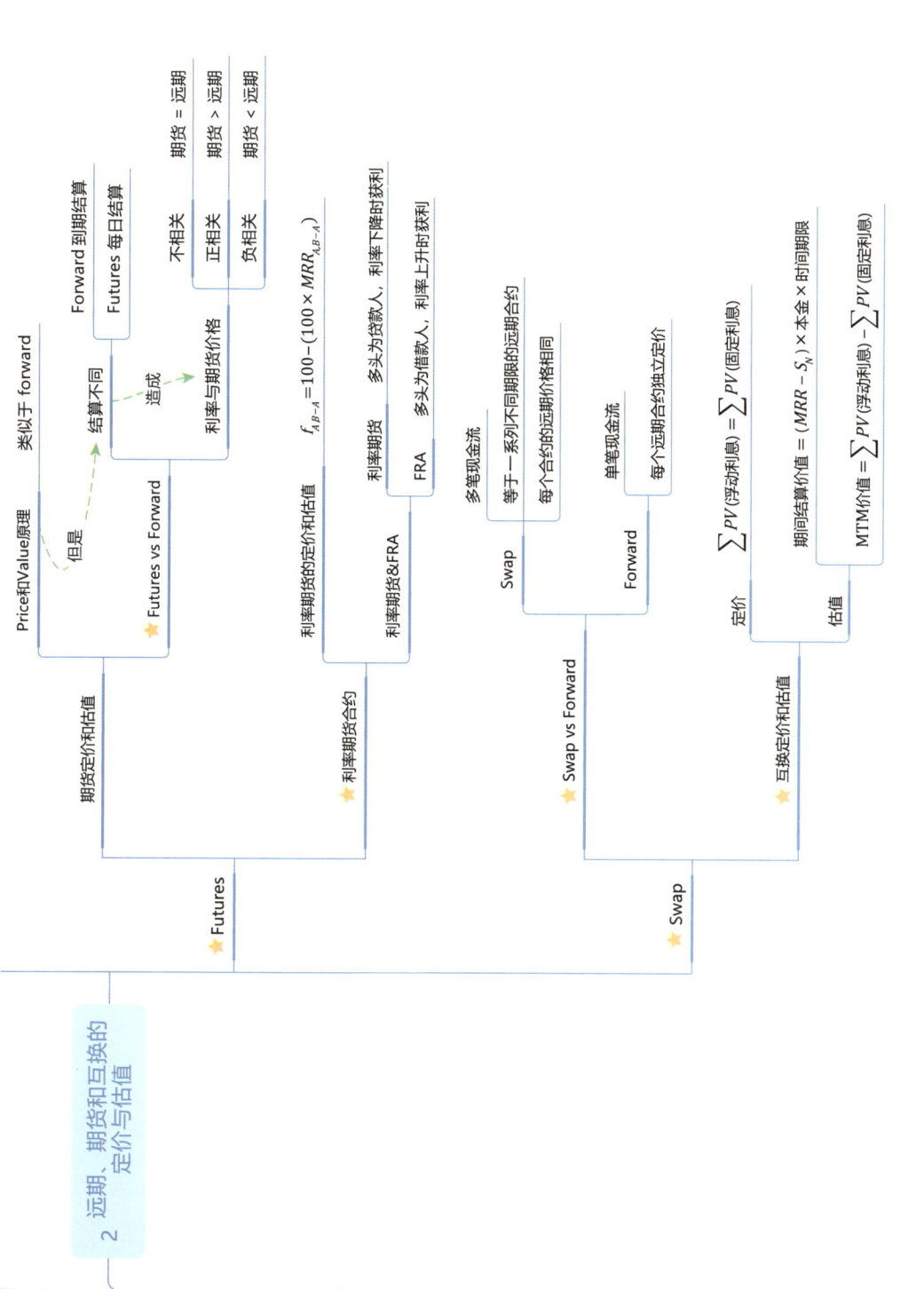

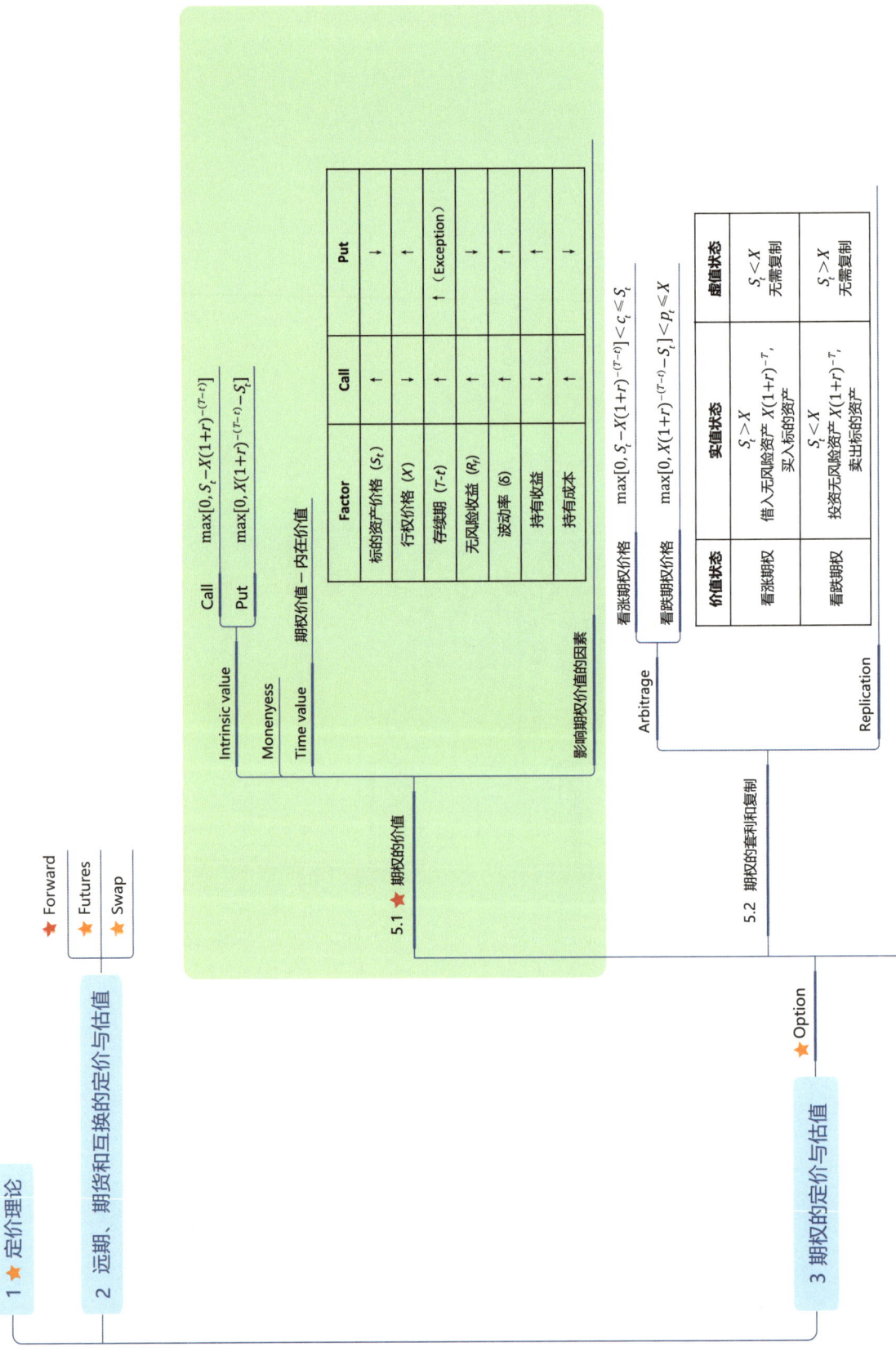

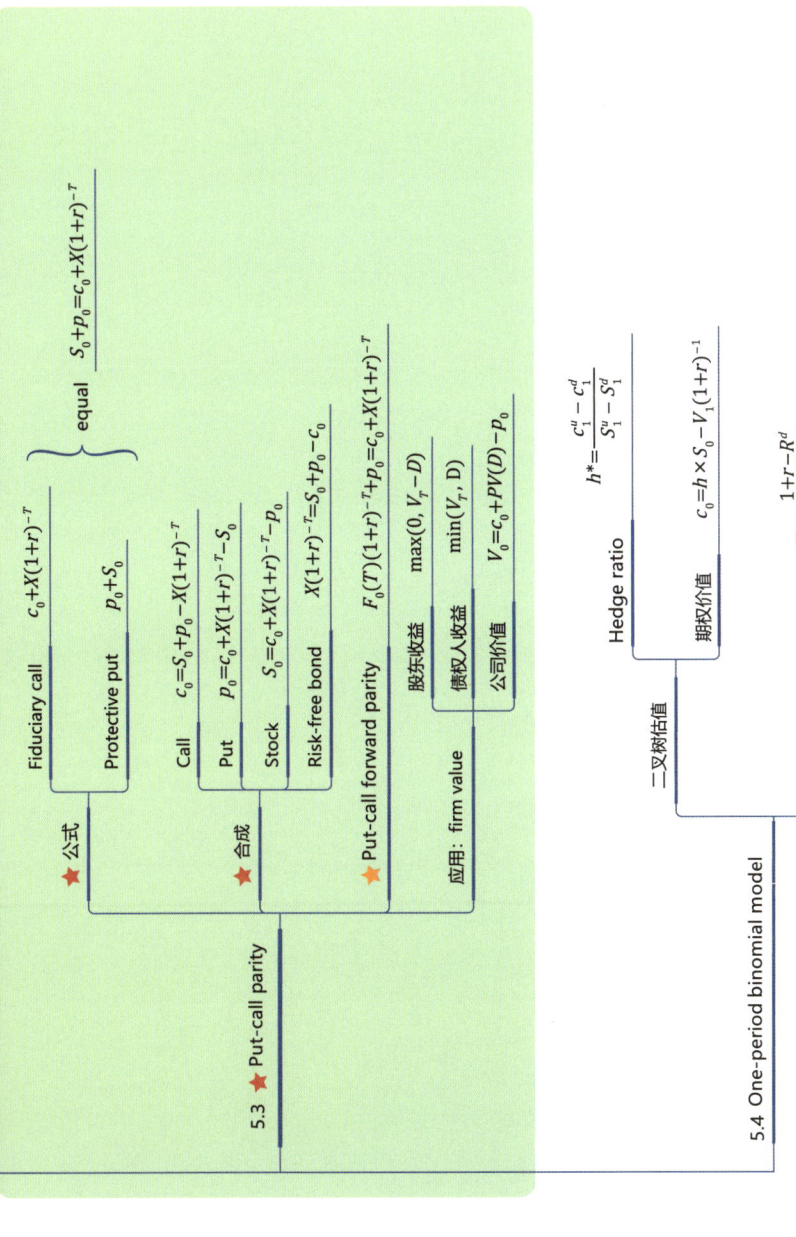

第八部分 另类投资

Reading 48　Basic Concepts of Alternative Investments

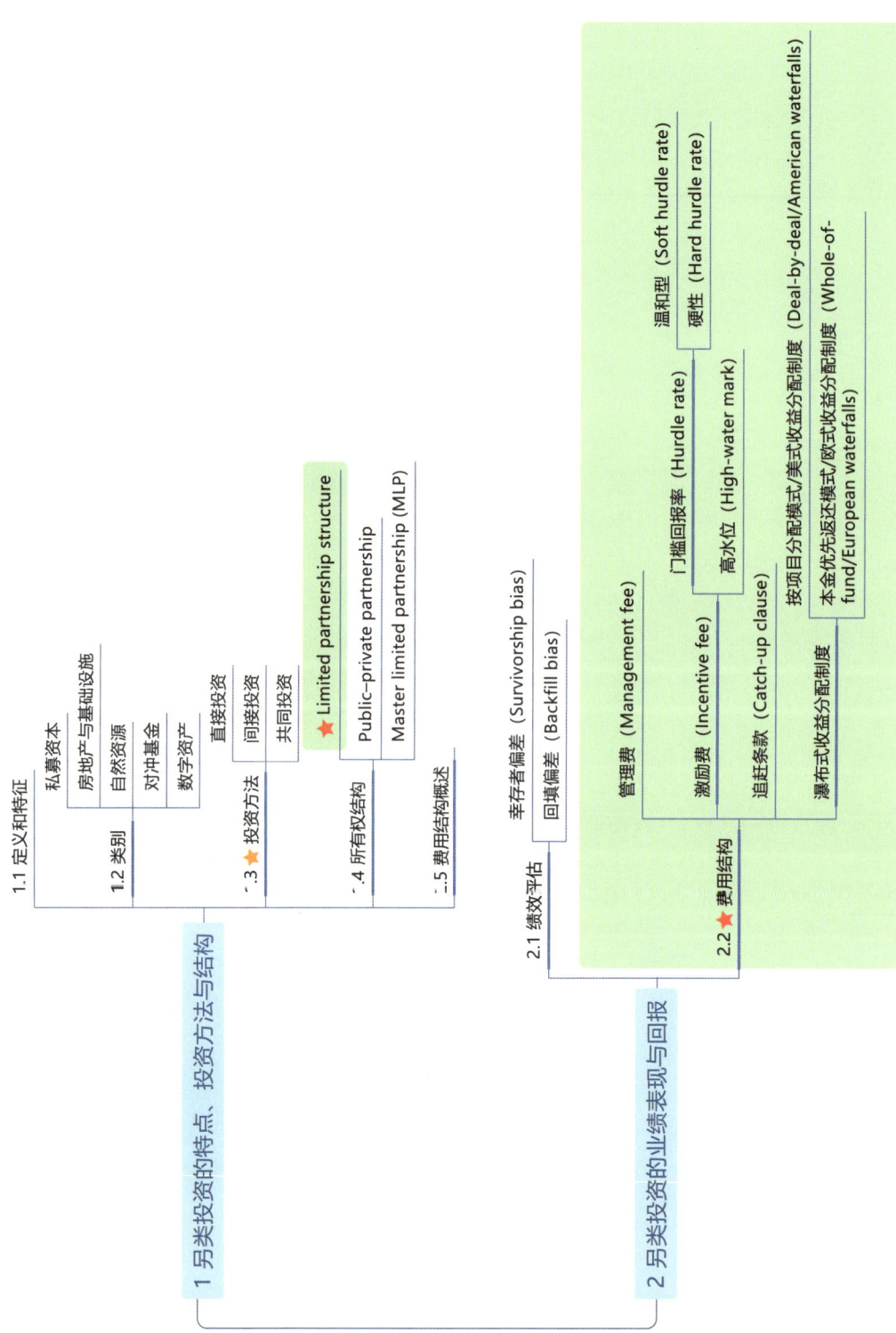

Reading 49 Asset Types of Alternative Investments

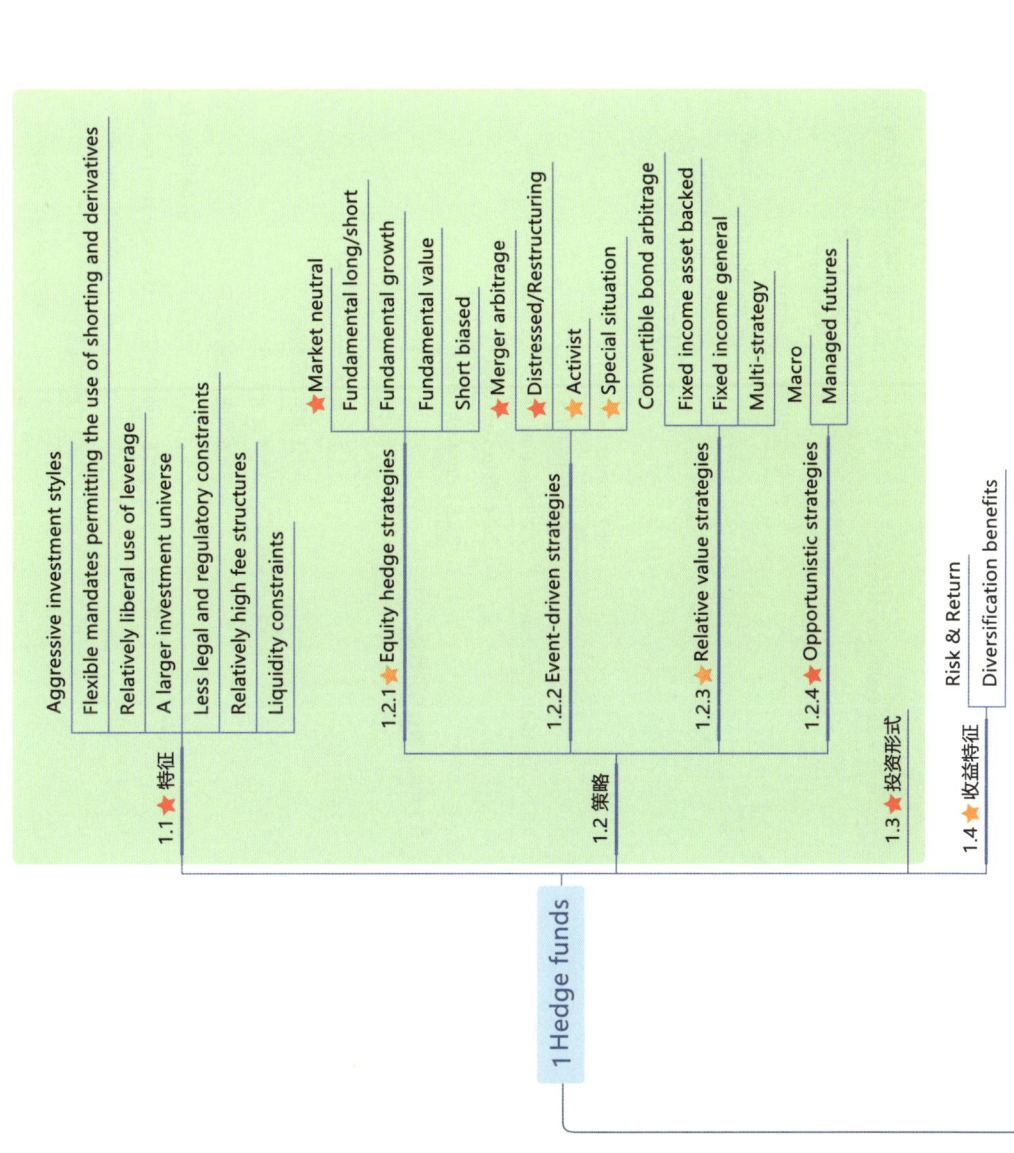

(见下页)

(见上页)

2 Private capital

2.1 ★ Private equity investment

2.1.1 类型
- Venture capital
- Growth capital
- Leveraged buyouts

2.1.2 退出机制
- IPO (Initial public offering)
- Direct listing
- Trade sale
- Secondary sale
- SPAC (Special purpose acquisition company)
- Write-off/Liquidation
- Recapitalization

2.2 Private debt investment
- 2.2.1 Direct lending
- 2.2.2 Mezzanine debt
- 2.2.3 Venture debt
- 2.2.4 Distressed debt
- 2.2.5 Unitranche debt

2.3 风险、收益与分散化

3 Real estate and infrastructure

3.1 Real estate
- 3.1.1 分类
- 3.1.2 ★ 特征
- 3.1.3 价格发现机制
- 3.1.4 ★ 投资方式
- 3.1.5 风险收益图谱
- 3.1.6 收益特征
  - Income generation & Capital appreciation
  - Diversification benefits: Low correlations with traditional assets
  - Consistent and steady cash flow reduces risk

3.2 Infrastructure
- 3.2.1 基本概念
- 3.2.2 ★ 分类
  - 基于标的资产的性质
  - 基于标的资产的发展阶段
- 3.2.3 投资形式

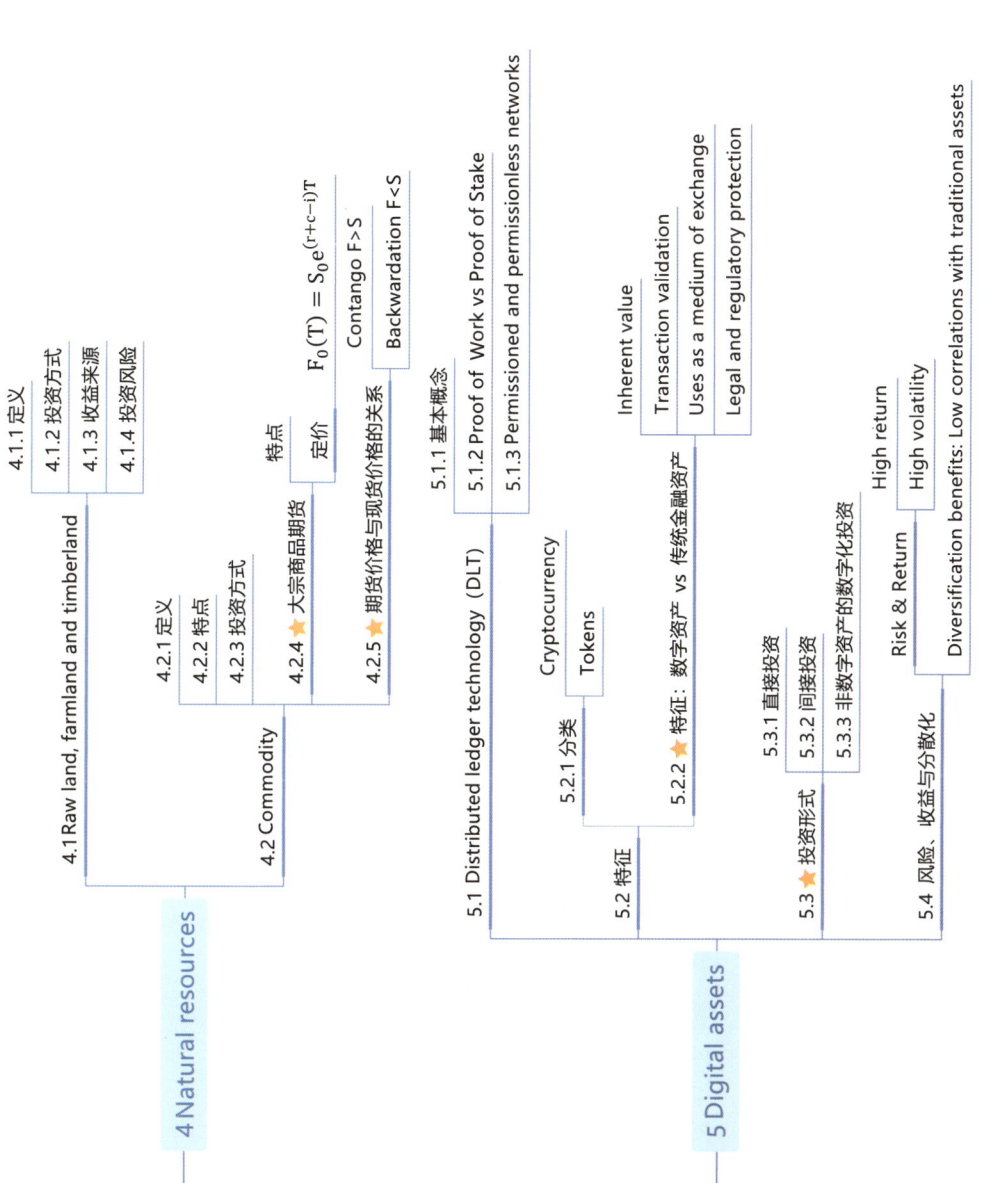

第九部分 投资组合管理

Reading 50　Portfolio Management: An Overview

1 ⭐ 组合管理的流程
- 1.1 Planning
  - Understanding objectives and constraints
  - Developing the investment policy statement (IPS)
    - Specifying the benchmark
    - Regularly reviewing IPS
- 1.2 Execution
  - Asset allocation
  - Security analysis
  - Portfolio construction trading and risk management
- 1.3 Feedback
  - Portfolio monitoring and rebalancing
  - Performance evaluation and reporting

2 投资者类型
- 2.1 Individual
- 2.2 ⭐ Institutional

Defined contribution (DC) pension plan

Institutional Investors	Time Horizon	Liquidity Needs	Risk Tolerance
DB pension plan	Long	Low	High
Endowments & Foundations	Long	Low	High
Banks	Short	High	Low
Insurance companies	Long for life; Short for P&C	High	Low

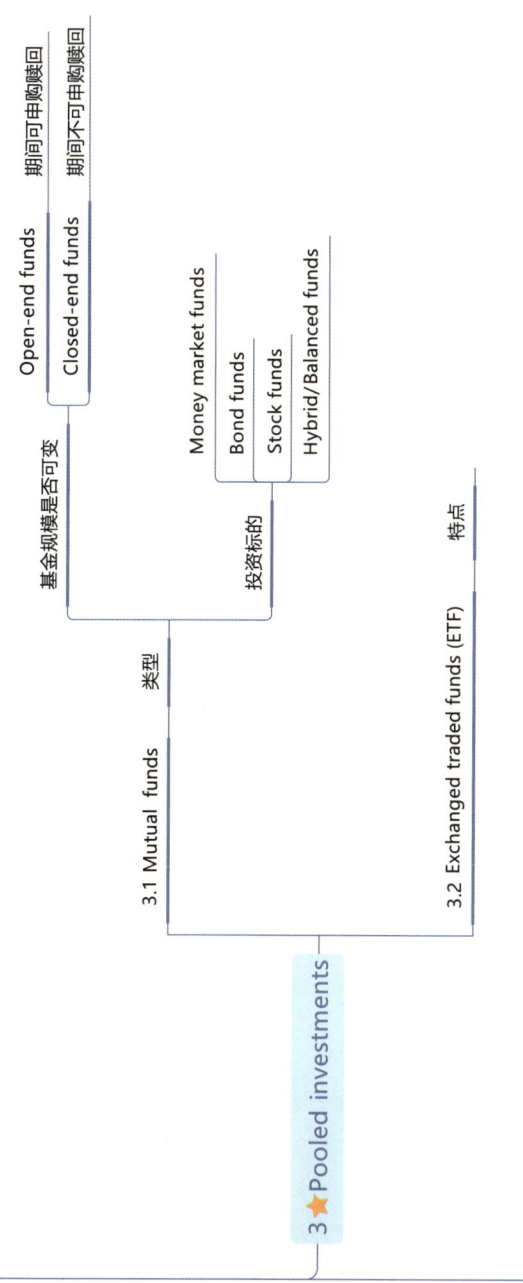

Reading 51　Portfolio Risk and Return: Part I

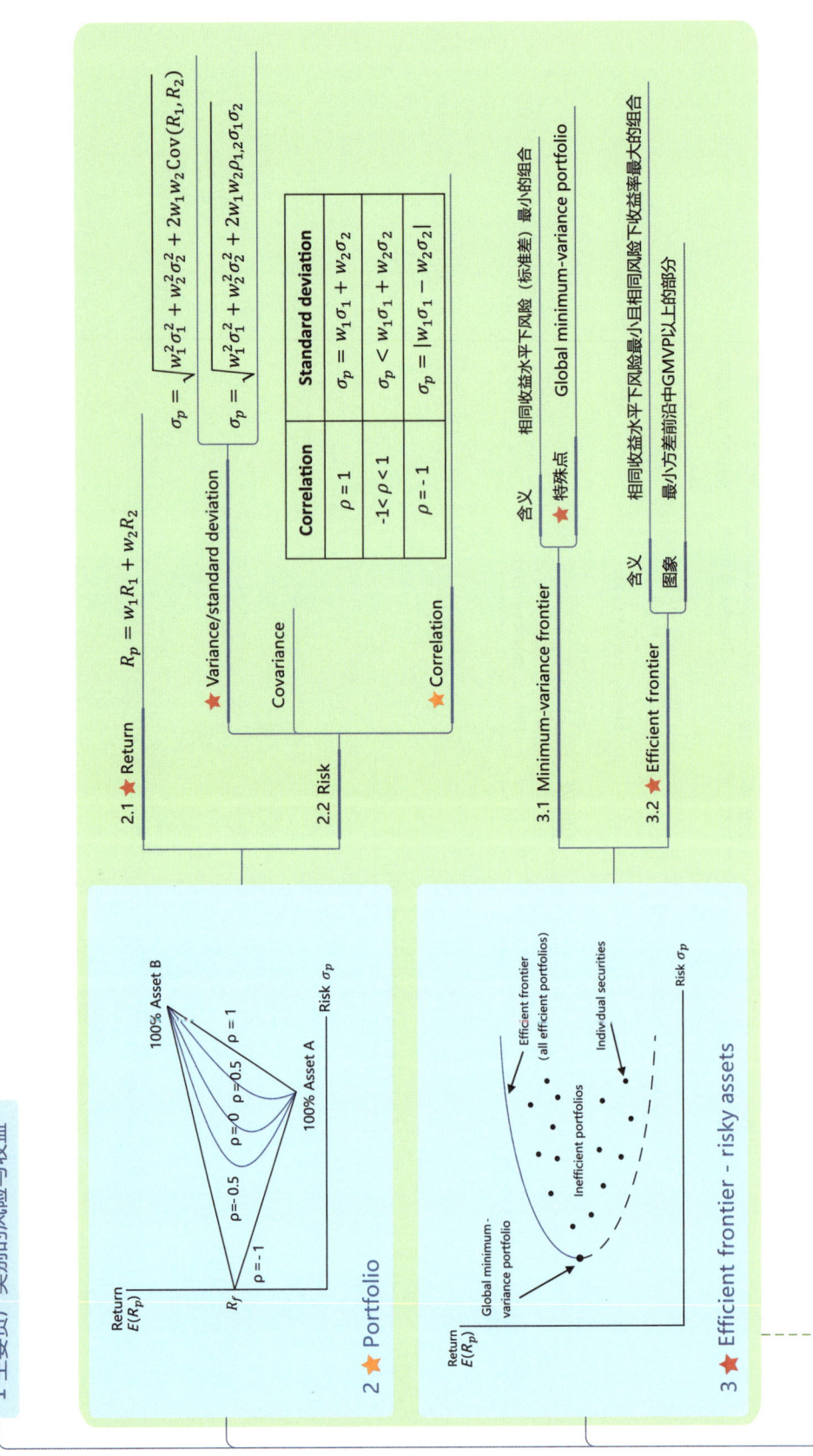

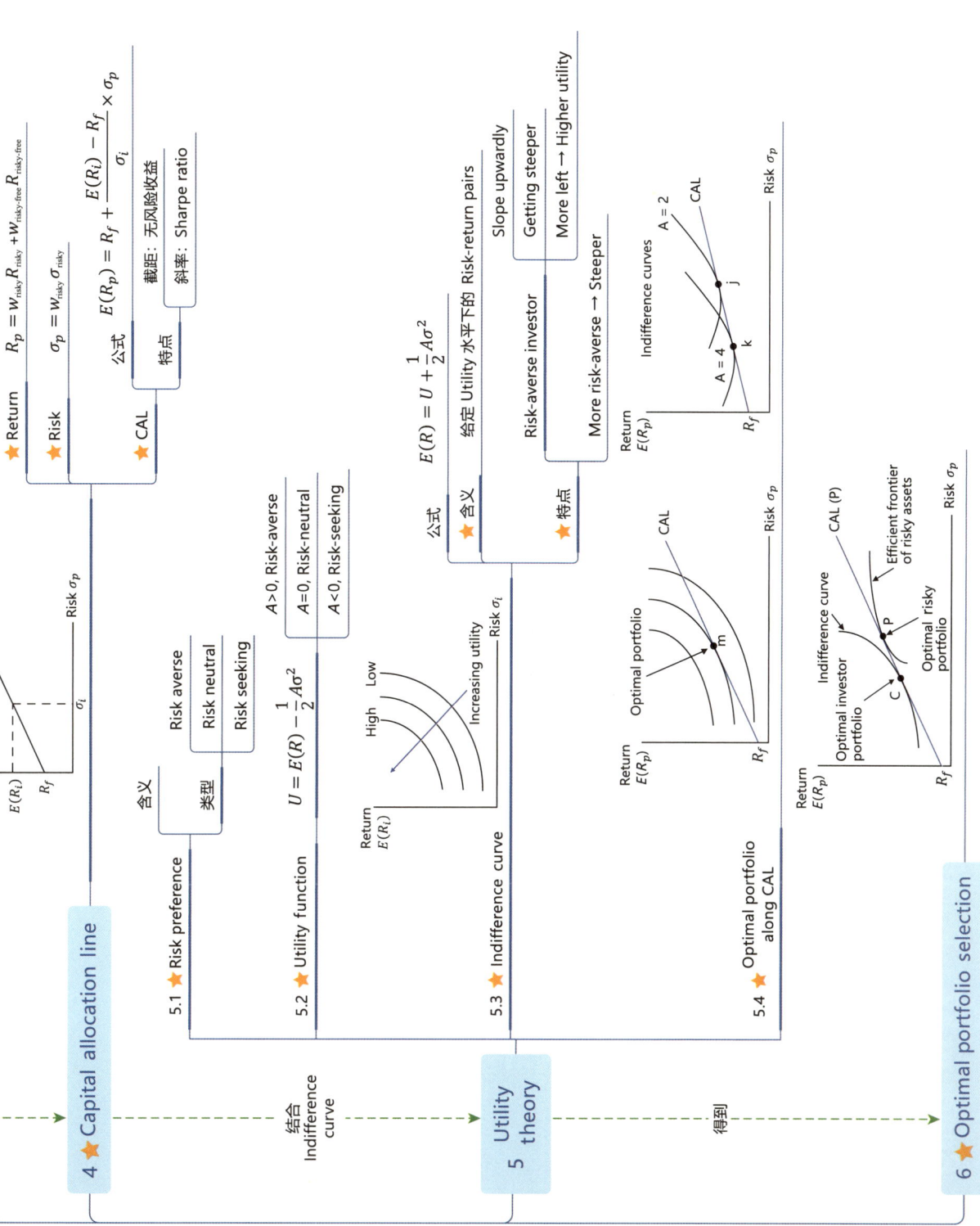

Reading 52 Portfolio Risk and Return: Part II

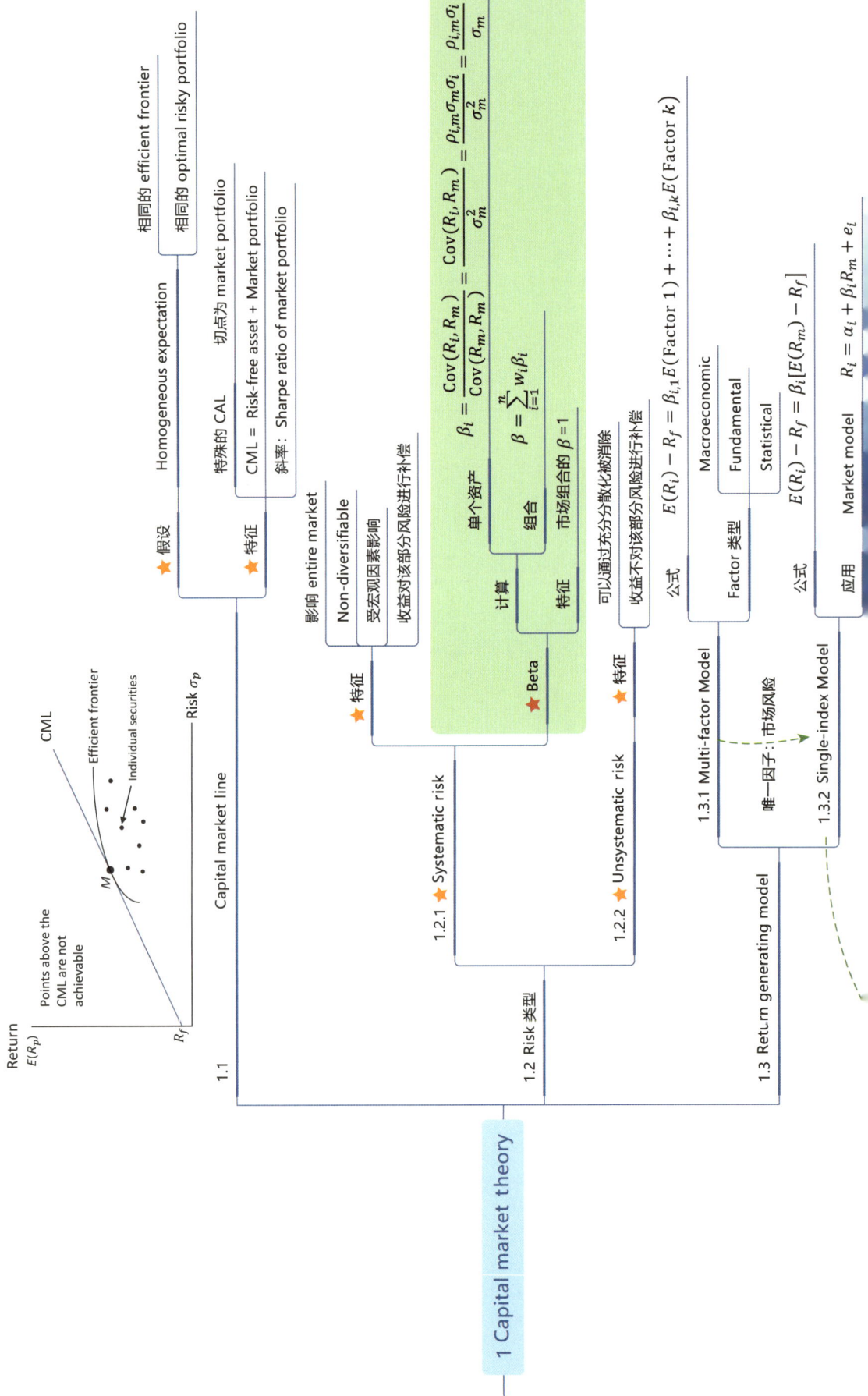

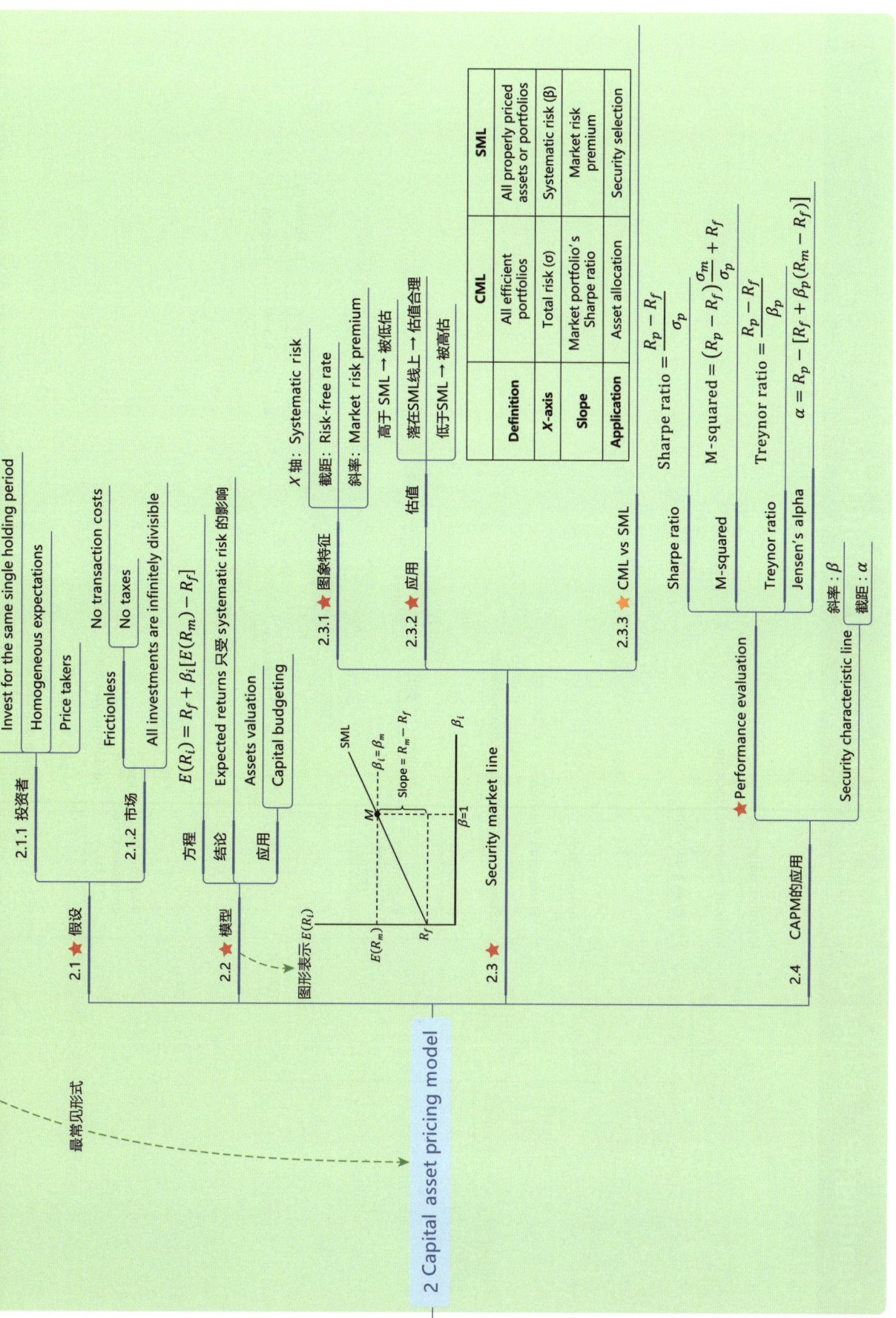

Reading 53　Basics of Portfolio Planning and Construction

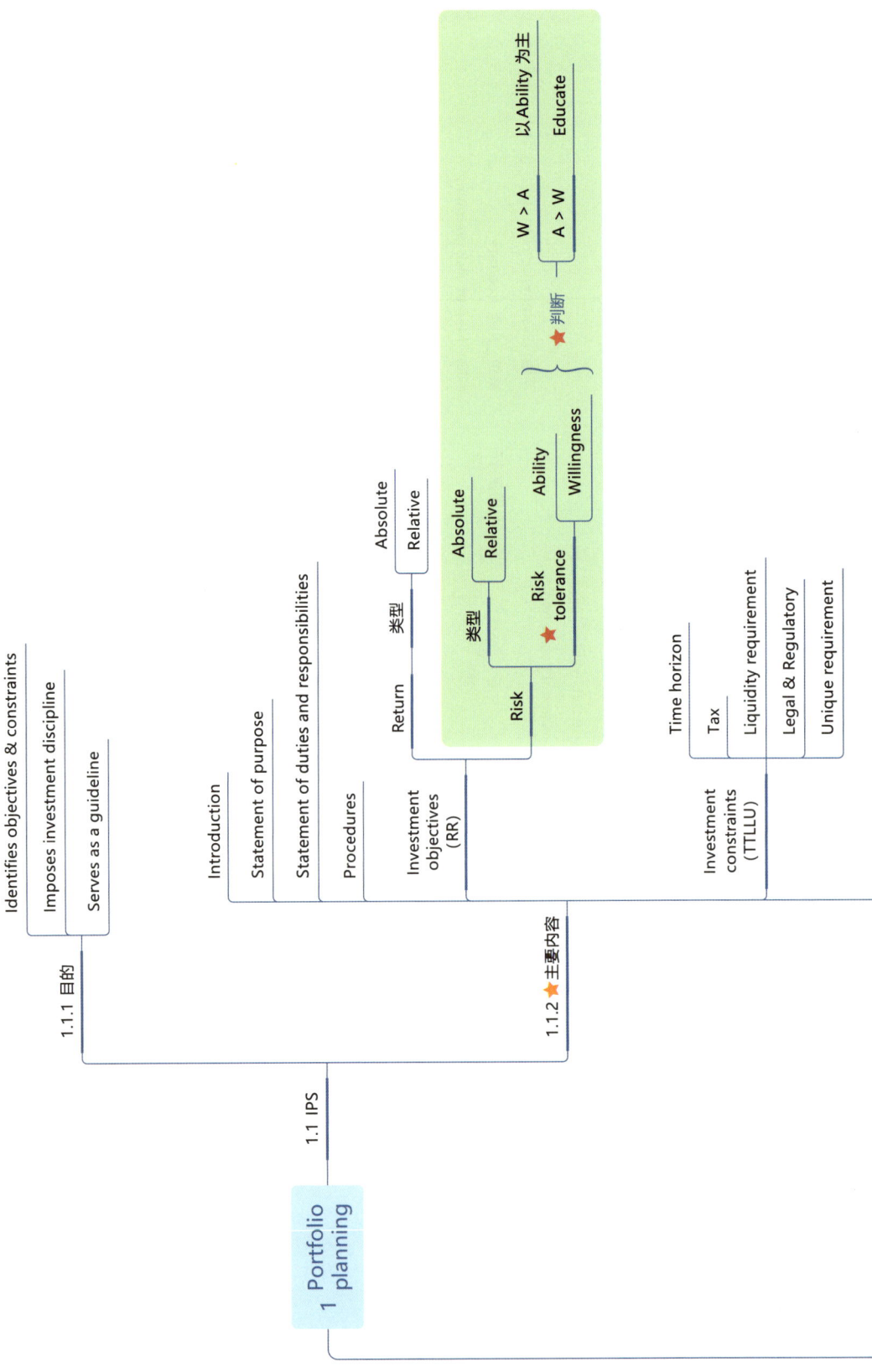

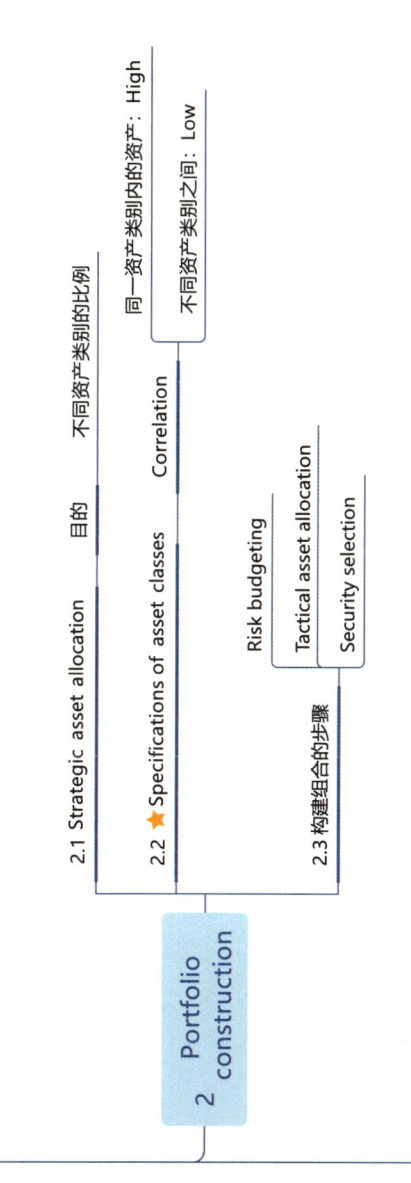

第九部分 投资组合管理 | 109

Reading 54　The Behavioral Biases of Individuals

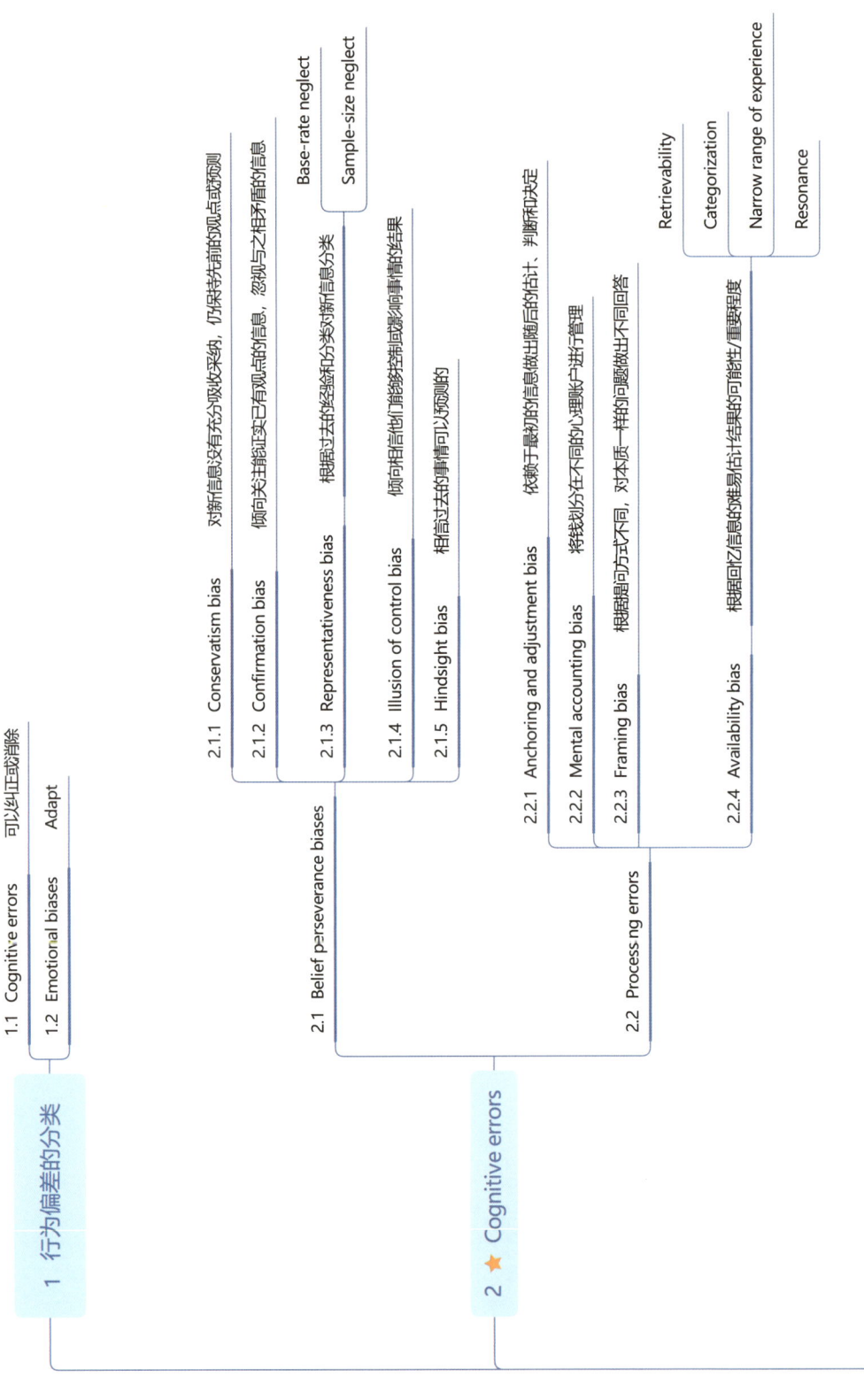

3 ⭐ Emotional biases

- **3.1 Loss-aversion bias** — 避免损失的强烈倾向 — Disposition effect
- **3.2 Overconfidence bias** — 表现出对自己能力毫无根据的信心
  - Prediction overconfidence
  - Certainty overconfidence
- **3.3 Self-control bias** — 缺乏自律，只追求近期的满足，而应对长期目标不采取行动
- **3.4 Status quo bias** — 保持现状，不做出改变
- **3.5 Endowment bias** — 拥有某项资产时，会比不拥有该资产时高估它的价值
- **3.6 Regret-aversion bias** — 害怕后悔，而避免做出任何决定 — Herding behavior

4 行为偏差对金融市场的影响

- 4.1 Market anomalies
- 4.2 Momentum
- 4.3 Bubbles and crashes
- 4.4 Value

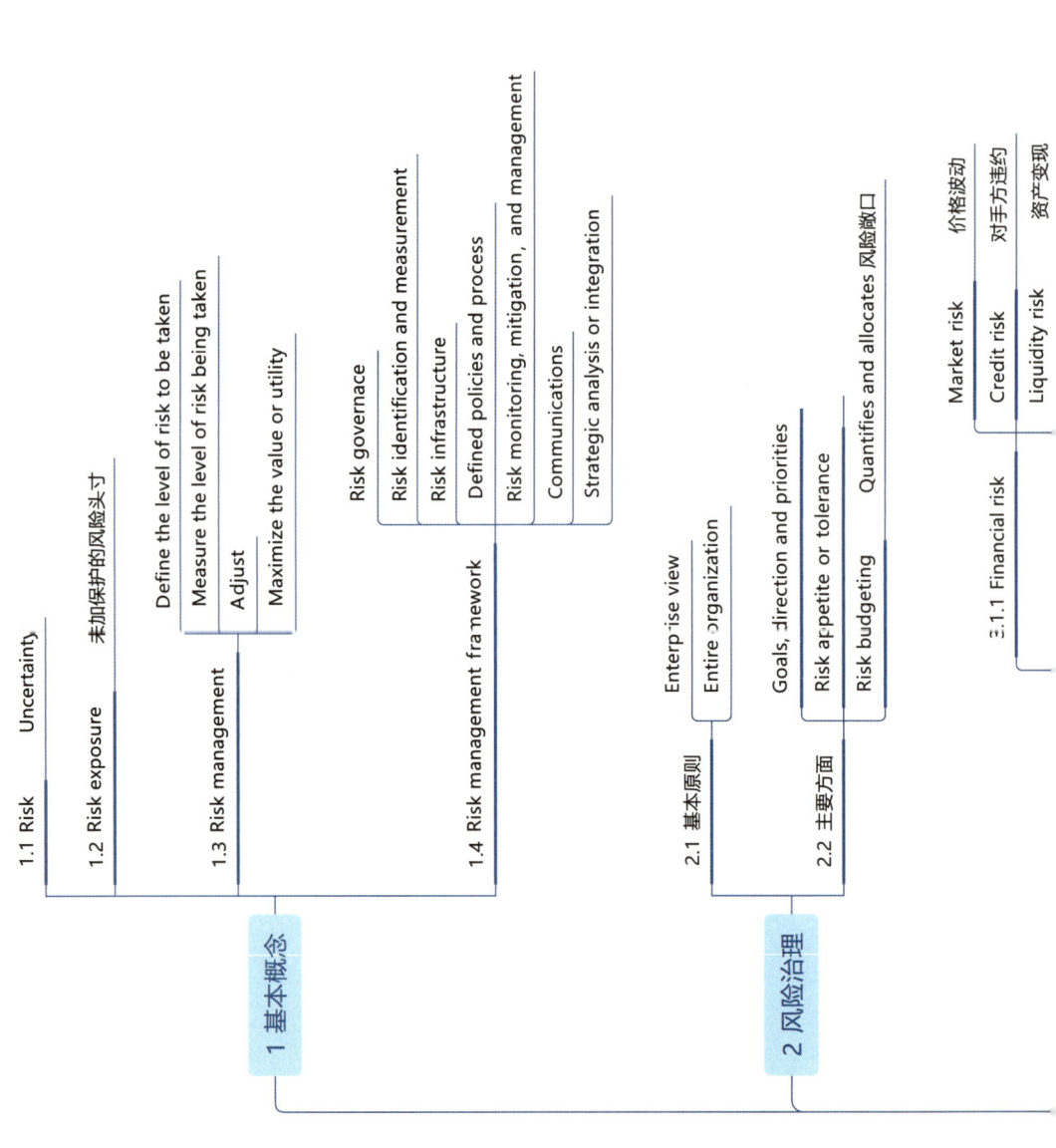

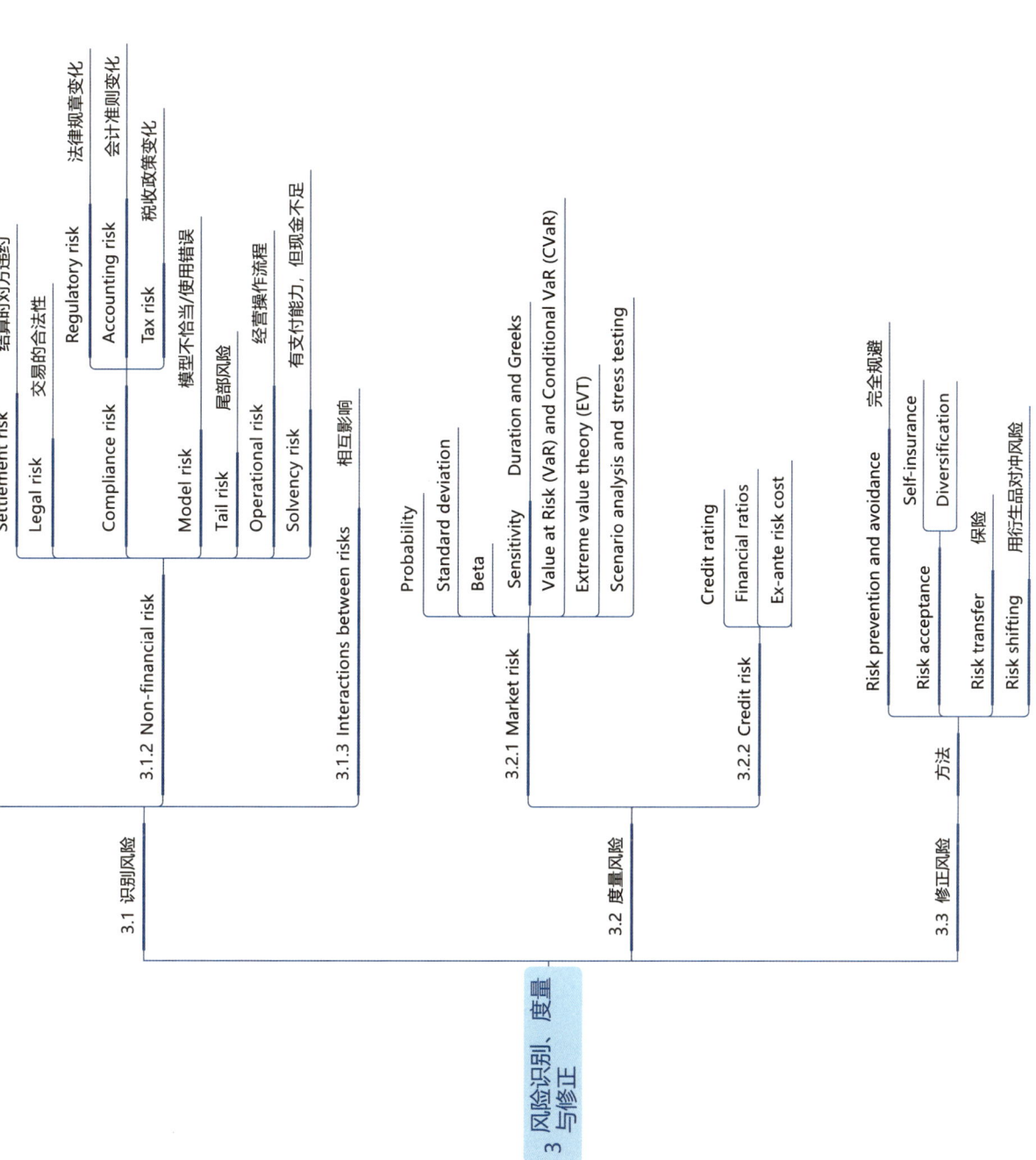

第十部分 伦理与职业标准

Reading 56 Ethics and Trust in the Investment Profession

1 道德的相关概念
- 1.1 Ethics — Moral/Ethical Principles
- 1.2 Code of ethics
  - Obligatory/Forbidden
  - General guide
- 1.3 Standards of conduct — Minimally acceptable behavior

2 职业与信任
- 2.1 职业的定义与特征
- 2.2 职业获取信任的方法

3 投资管理中的专业性
- 3.1 投资管理中的信任
- 3.2 投资管理专业组织：CFA®协会

4 ★ 道德行为的挑战
- 4.1 Overconfidence
- 4.2 Situational influences

5 道德与法律的辨析
- ★ 关系 — 既可交叉，也存在冲突 (Legal & Ethical; Legal; Ethical)
- ★ 法律并不是约束不道德行为的最佳机制

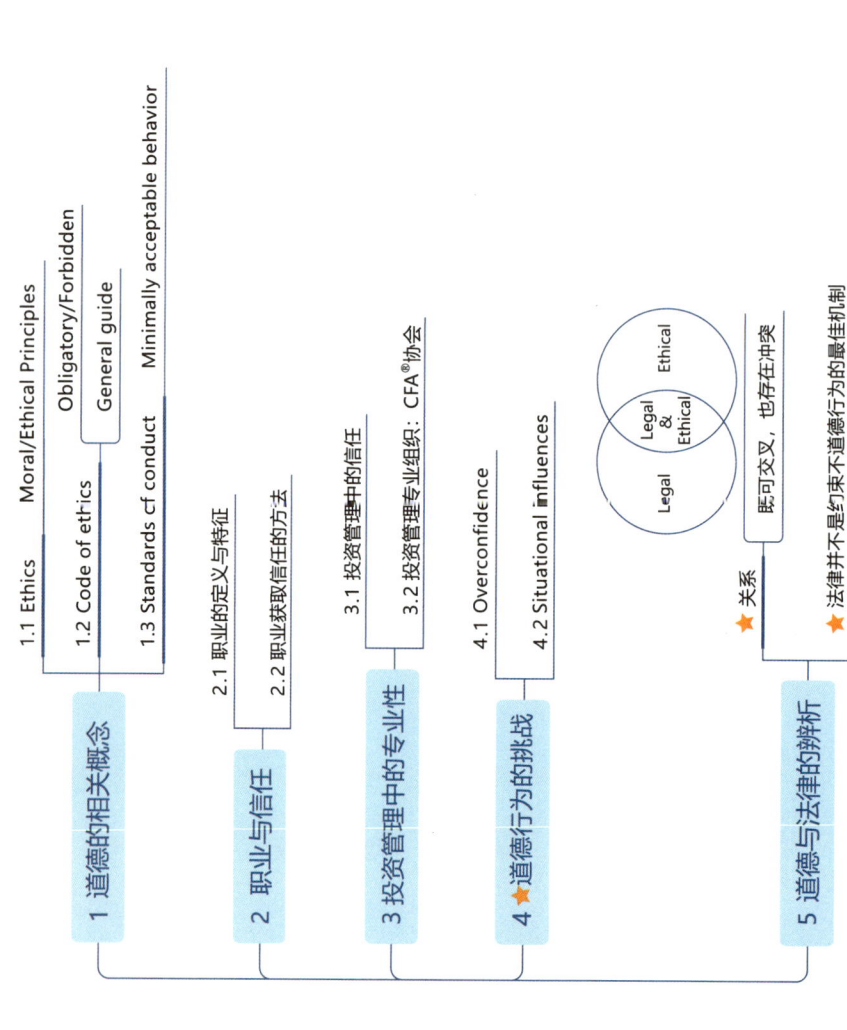

Reading 57 Code of Ethics and Standards of Professional Conduct

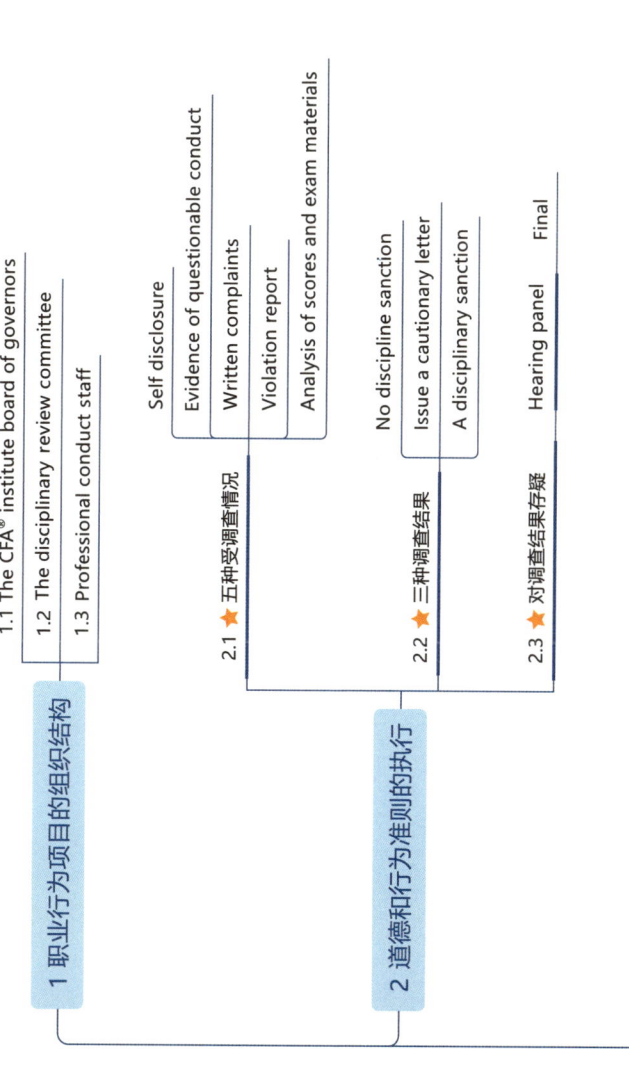

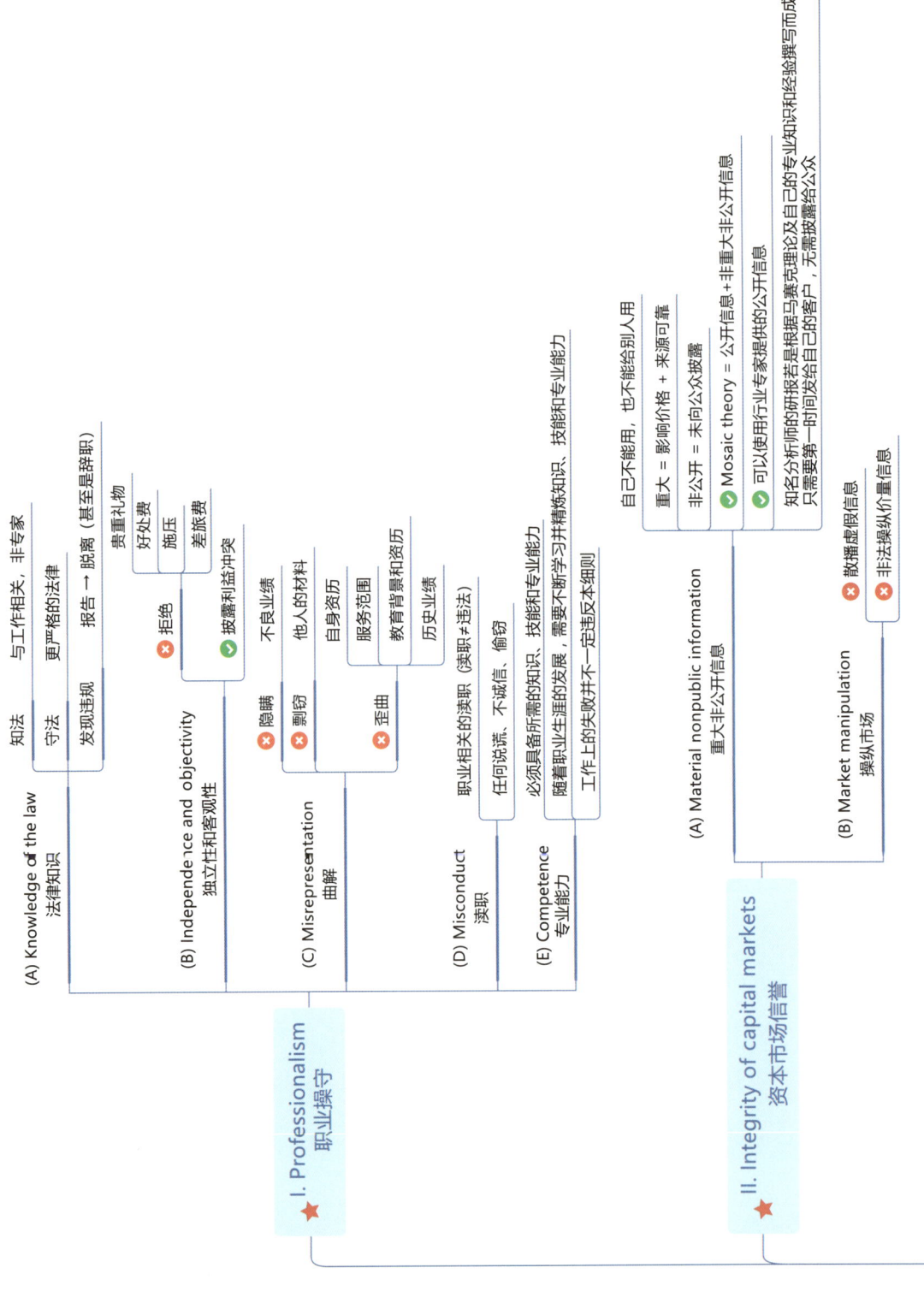

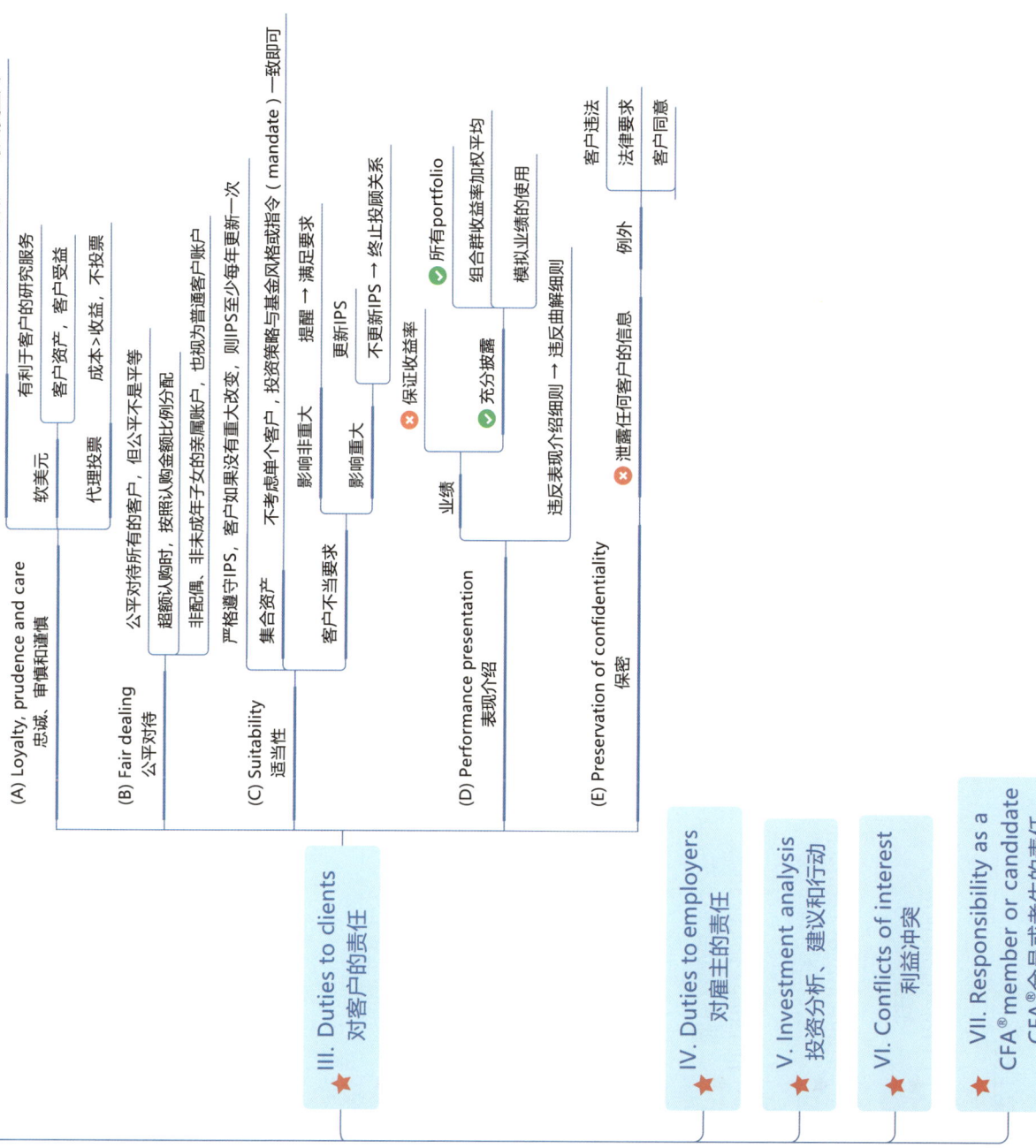

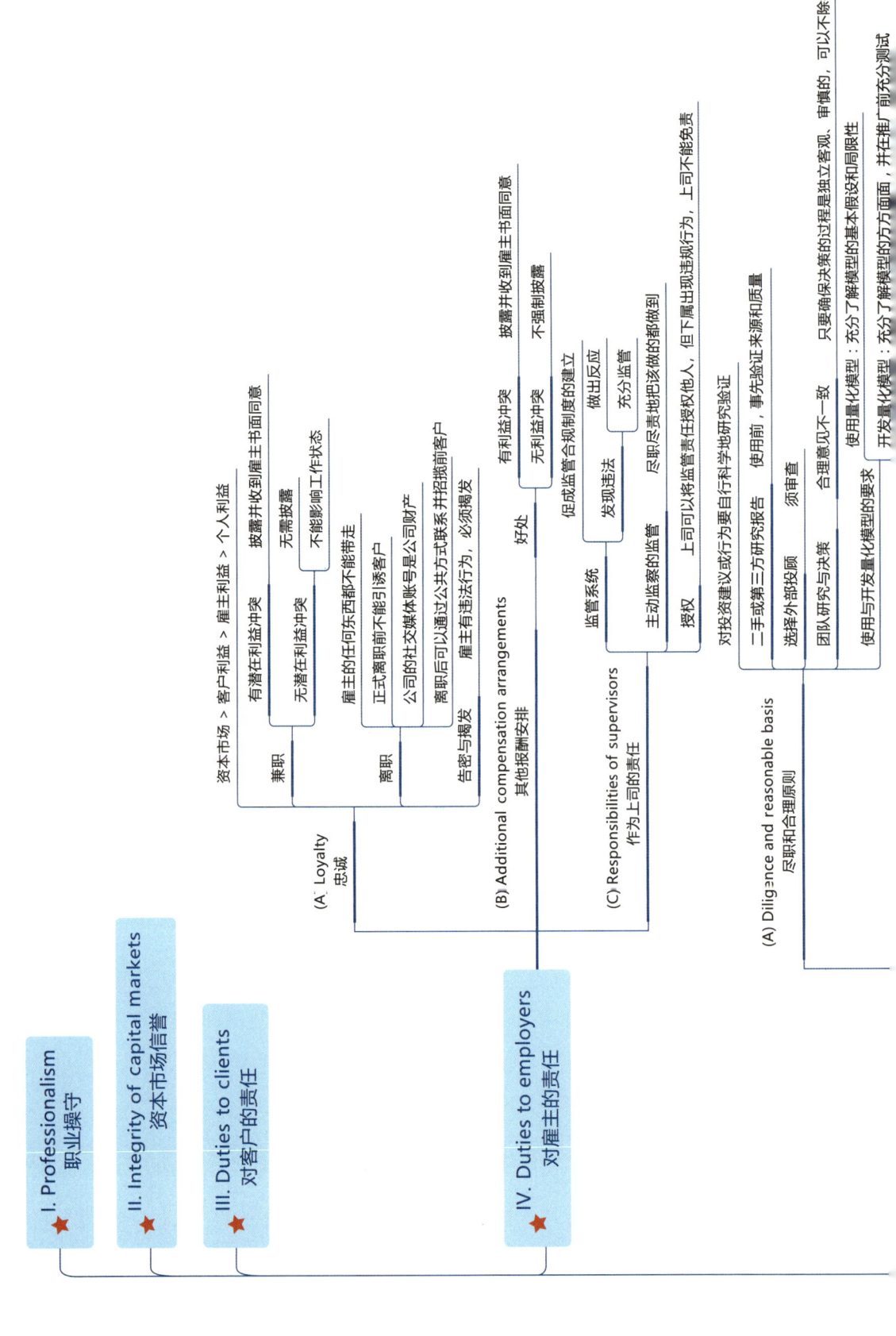

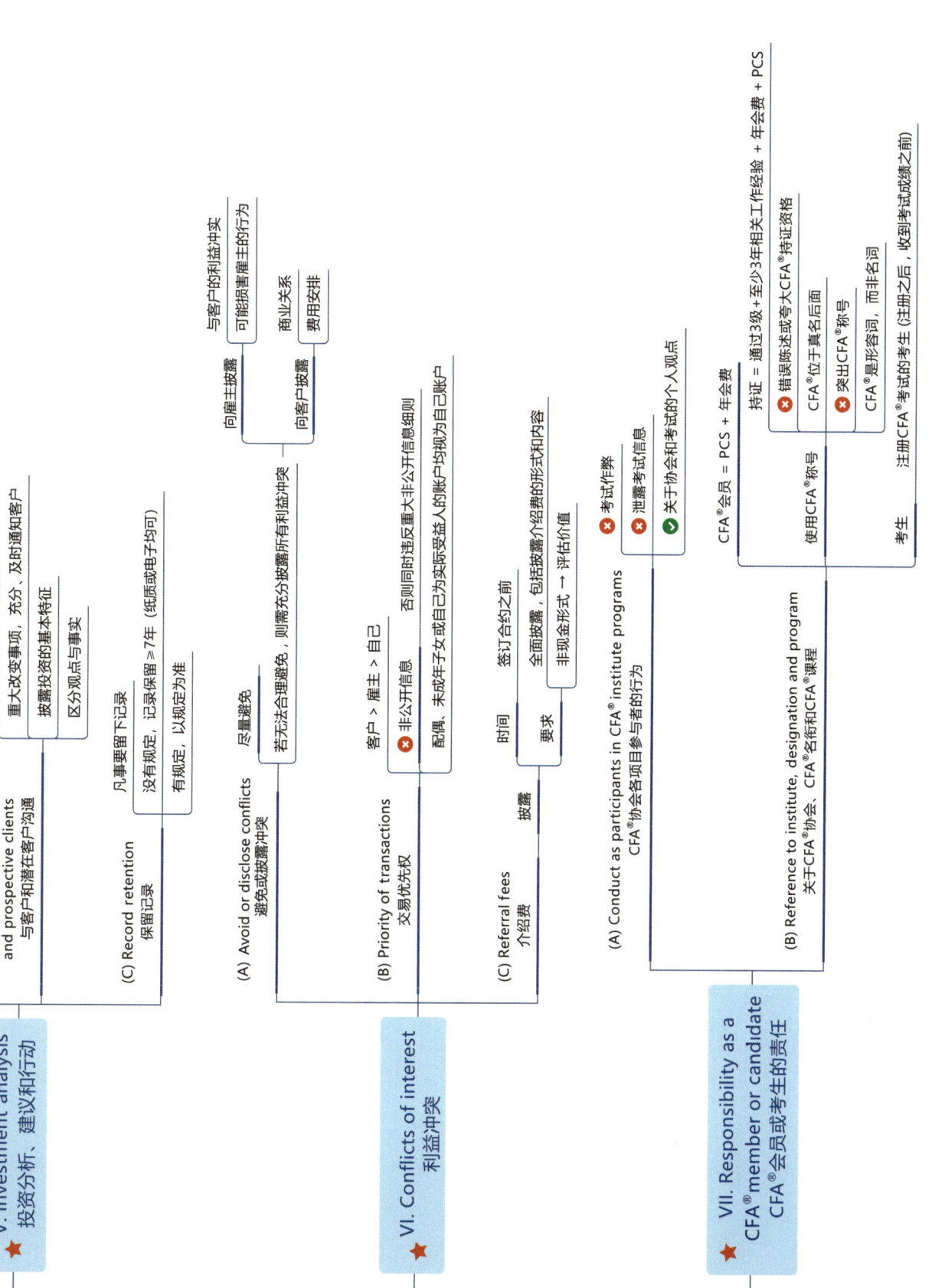

Reading 59 Introduction to the Global Investment Performance Standards (GIPS)

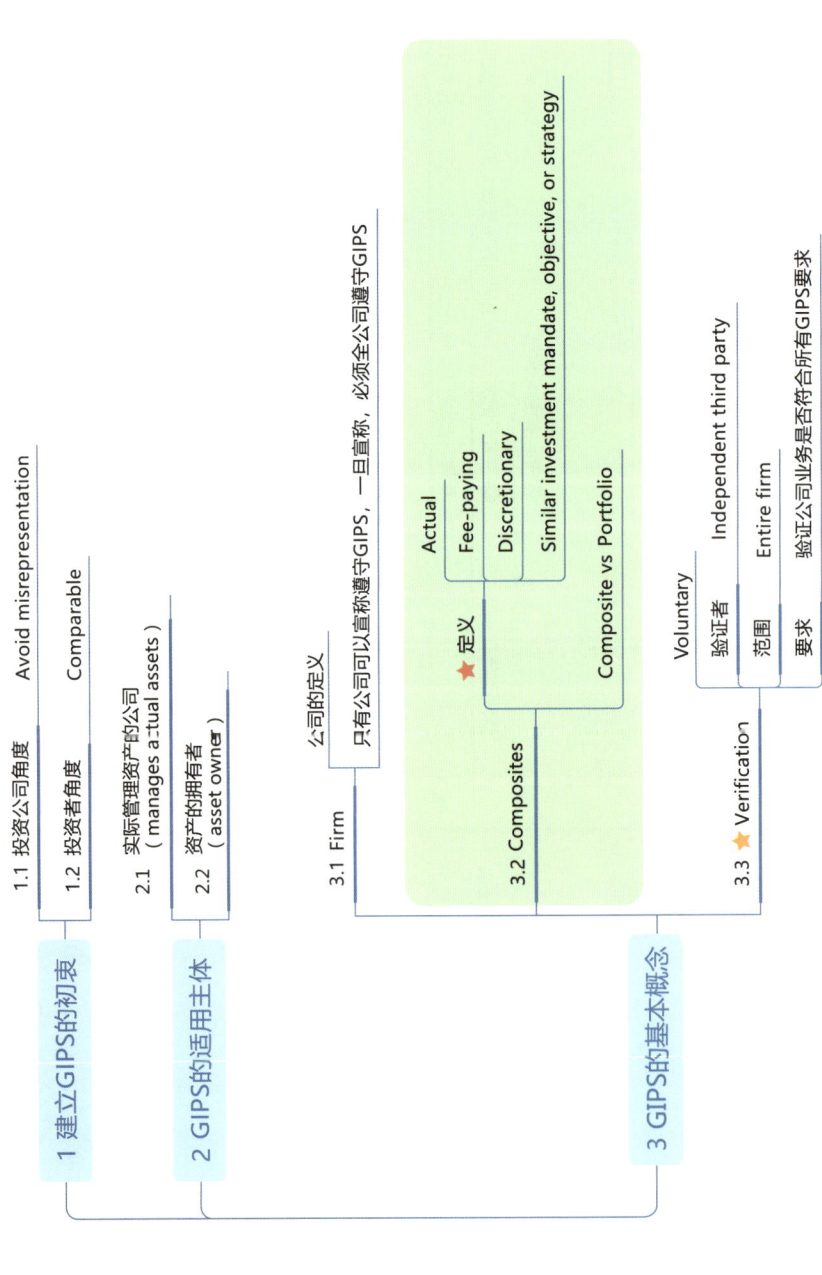

Reading 60 Ethics Application

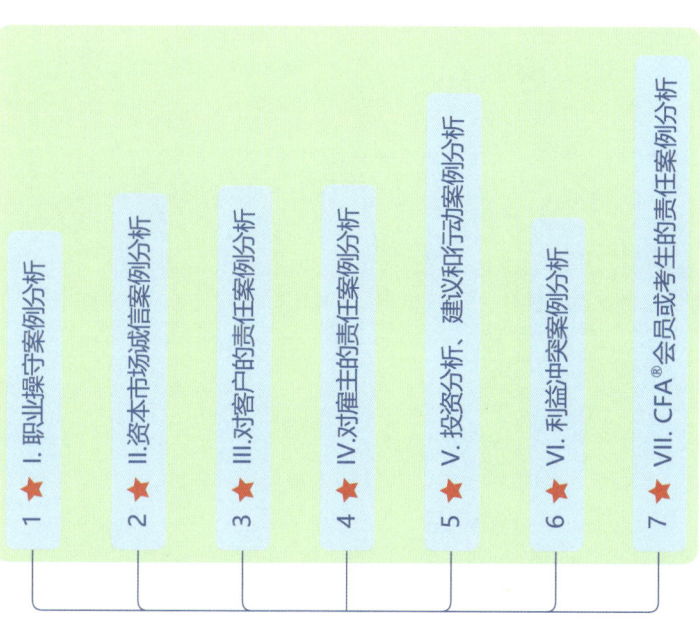

扫码即可反馈对本书的使用意见并查看在线勘误